Welcome to

THE
EVERYTHING

PARENT'S GUIDES

As a parent, you're swamped with conflicting advice and parenting techniques that tell you what is best for your child. THE EVERYTHING® PARENT'S GUIDES get right to the point about specific issues. They give you the most recent, up-to-date information on parenting trends, behavior issues, and health concerns—providing you with a detailed resource to help you ease your parenting anxieties.

THE EVERYTHING® PARENT'S GUIDES are an extension of the bestselling Everything® series in the parenting category. These family-friendly books are designed to be a one-stop guide for parents. If you want authoritative information on specific topics not fully covered in other books, THE EVERYTHING® PARENT'S GUIDES are the perfect resource to ensure that you raise a healthy, confident child.

Visit the entire Everything® se

D1218494

THE EVERYTHING

PARENT'S GUIDE TO

Raising Boys

Dear Reader,

Early one May morning twenty-one years ago, my son was born. His father and I were delighted: He was a healthy, smiling baby and quickly grew into an inquisitive, charming toddler. Parenting was a snap, I thought—and then he turned three. I quickly discovered that what I knew about raising a boy—habits and ideas I'd gleaned from my own upbringing, plus miscellaneous bits of information gathered from friends and relatives—didn't work very well with the real-life son I had.

My own mission to learn more about parenting (particularly about parenting boys) led me eventually to a master's degree in marriage and family therapy and nine books on parenting, two of which deal specifically with boys. I have been a single mom and part of a stepfamily. My boy is now on his own and enjoying life immensely; I celebrate his successes and miss him every day.

Raising a son is a wonderful adventure; it can also be quite a challenge. Yet I believe with all my heart that nothing you do will be as important (or as rewarding) as raising your son. While I do not claim to know all the answers, the volume you hold in your hands contains tried-and-true information from many sources, as well as cutting-edge knowledge about how boys grow and develop.

Your son is lucky to have a parent who cares enough to learn more about raising him. Enjoy your journey together!

Cheryl L. Erwin

THE

EVERYTHING®

PARENT'S GUIDE TO

RAISING BOYS

A complete handbook to develop
confidence, promote self-esteem,
and improve communication

Cheryl L. Erwin

Adams Media
Avon, Massachusetts

This book is dedicated to the memory of my father,
Donald W. Gresser, who demonstrated by his own life
what it means to be a good man.

• • •

Publishing Director: Gary M. Krebs
Associate Managing Editor: Laura M. Daly
Associate Copy Chief: Brett Palana-Shanahan
Acquisitions Editor: Kate Burgo
Development Editor: Rachel Engelson
Associate Production Editor: Casey Ebert

Director of Manufacturing: Susan Beale
Associate Director of Production:
Michelle Roy Kelly
Cover Design: Paul Beatrice, Matt LeBlanc,
Erick DaCosta
Design and Layout: Colleen Cunningham,
Sorae Lee, Jennifer Oliveira

An Everything® Series Book.
Everything® and everything.com® are registered trademarks of F+W Publications, Inc.

Published by Adams Media, an F+W Publications Company
57 Littlefield Street, Avon, MA 02322 U.S.A.
www.adamsmedia.com

ISBN: 1-59337-587-5

Printed in the United States of America.

J I H G F E D C B A

Library of Congress Cataloging-in-Publication Data
Erwin, Cheryl.
The everything parent's guide to raising boys / Cheryl L. Erwin.
p.   cm.
Includes bibliographical references.
ISBN 1-59337-587-5
1. Boys. 2. Parenting. 3. Child rearing. I. Title. II. Series.
HQ775.E79 2006
649'.132--dc22
                                        2006005016

This book is available at quantity discounts for bulk purchases.
For information, please call 1-800-872-5627.

boy (boi) ▶ n. **1.** A bundle of energy combined with boundless curiosity, a surprisingly soft heart, and a dash of independence. When blended well with love, laughter, patience, and thoughtful teaching, over time will become one fine young man.

Acknowledgments

The Everything® Parent's Guide to Raising Boys is rooted in the work of Alfred Adler and Rudolf Dreikurs, pioneers of the idea that parenting is not only a science but a skill that can be learned. I am indebted to my dear friend Jane Nelsen and my many Positive Discipline colleagues, who have devoted their lives to creating respectful, caring families, schools, and communities.

I also want to express my deep gratitude to Jody for listening, to Philip for being my best teacher, and to David for loving support, great background music, and lots of patience.

• • •

Contents

Introduction

Few things in life are as important as raising a child. Parents dream of the birth of a baby; they read stacks of books and magazine articles, attend classes, and talk eagerly with other parents. They mull over names and cherish hopes about whether their child will be a boy or a girl. Then the baby—a real, flesh-and-blood boy—arrives. Suddenly nothing is as clear and simple as it once seemed.

The realities of raising a boy take even the most loving, committed, educated parents by surprise. At first, the challenges are fairly straightforward: You want him to eat, to sleep, and occasionally, to give you a moment's peace. You must figure out the rhythms of his tiny body and how to soothe him. When your son isn't crying, he is adorable.

He makes interesting noises, grins disarmingly, and becomes the subject of nearly every conversation you have. You can watch him sleep for hours, your heart filled with wonder. Photographs begin to litter the walls and tabletops, and toys and the other accessories of childhood take over entire rooms of your home.

Sooner or later, though, the precious infant becomes a little boy (and then a bigger boy). He develops a personality of his own. He finds interesting new ways to explore his world. He makes messes and gets into trouble. And occasionally, he proves not to be exactly what (or who) you expected. Most parents—indeed, most cultures in the world—have a set of expectations and ideals that go with the word "male." Yet, as you will discover, much of what people sometimes take for granted about boys is not entirely accurate.

Boys, as it turns out, are not like girls—especially during the early years of their lives. They learn differently and have different strengths; they sometimes need different things from parents. In addition to understanding just how your son's gender affects his development and behavior, you must learn all of the other skills and ideas that parents must master.

You must provide consistent discipline, learn to offer and invite open communication, and teach your boy the skills and character he needs in order to thrive in life. You must help him develop a healthy sense of self-esteem, build friendships and relationships with others, and succeed in school. You must decide when to say yes and when to say no and whether to pamper and protect him or allow him to struggle a bit on his own. Most importantly, you must learn to know both your son and yourself well enough to make the life-shaping decisions that lie ahead of you.

You may have noticed that advice on how to raise your boy abounds. Bookstore shelves groan with parenting books. Self-proclaimed experts offer advice on television and radio programs, while entire magazines are devoted to parenting tips and suggestions. Raising your son is so important: How will you know what to do?

No one will ever know your boy like you do. Information about parenting is a good thing, but you must learn to trust your own wisdom and knowledge of your son to make the right decisions about the challenges you face together. You must decide what you want for your son and be willing to follow through every day of your lives together.

You most certainly love your son, but love is not always enough to raise a child well. You must learn to mix love with wisdom, good judgment, and self-control. You will discover that doing the right thing as a parent sometimes does not feel very good, that saying no (even when you know you should) can be painful for you and the boy you love. Wise parents learn to rely on both their heads and their hearts, to ask for help when they need it, and to be willing to learn from their own mistakes.

The Everything Parent's Guide to Raising Boys offers you information, suggestions, and stories of parents much like you. It can, with your own wisdom and experience, help you raise a successful, capable, happy young man.

CHAPTER 1

It's a Boy!

Gather any group of expectant parents together, and you're likely to hear one or two questions over and over: "Do you know what you're having?" or perhaps, "What do you really want?" These parents aren't discussing a dinner menu; when you prepare to have a baby, gender matters. There are names to select and clothing and bedding to buy, but the gender of your baby involves far more than fashion choices. Once the big day has come, and you have a son, what do you need to know?

Why Does Gender Matter?

Psychologist Elaine Aron, Ph.D., tells the story of an informal experiment on gender. A young infant was left in a park with an attendant who claimed to have agreed to sit with the baby for a few minutes, not knowing if it was a boy or a girl. Many people stopped to admire the infant, and every one of them was upset about not knowing the baby's gender. Several even volunteered to undress the baby to find out.

Gender forms one of the earliest expectations parents have for their children. Some parents pray for a son; others hope for a girl. Why? Are boys and girls really that different?

Until recently, even researchers were reluctant to talk much about gender differences. In the world of women's liberation and political correctness, there was something suspicious about saying that girls and boys might be inherently different. Parents were encouraged to avoid gender bias and were discouraged from teaching stereotypes to their sons and daughters. Little girls should not be restricted to dolls, this reasoning went; instead, they should be encouraged to become police officers and doctors, not "just mommies."

Little boys faced an even more difficult challenge. You may agree that it is good for girls to explore their strengths, but is it really all right for boys to explore their sensitivity? The same parent who chuckles as his son tumbles around the playground, shaking his head and saying with a smile, "Boys will be boys," may feel a small stab of worry when that same little boy picks up his sister's doll and contentedly settles down to play.

Much of what you have learned about boys and girls comes from generations of assumptions, from your own parents, from your friends, and from the world around you. For example, you may believe that boys are strong while girls are weaker. Boys are brave; girls are more timid. Girls cook and clean; boys go to work to provide for girls. Girls are allowed to cry; boys had better not cry in public.

Society allows girls to be giddy and silly; boys must demonstrate that they know how to be manly. Even in this liberated world, working women still bear the bulk of the responsibility for child care, keeping a home, cooking, and cleaning. Why? Well, our culture still assumes that those jobs are women's work. Many mothers never train their sons to do these tasks.

As you hold your own precious son in your arms or watch him begin to explore the world around him, you may find yourself wondering exactly what it means to raise a son. What is masculinity, anyway? What do you need to know to raise a healthy, happy boy, one who grows up to be a healthy, happy man?

Are Boys Different from Girls?

In 1967, twin boys were born to a family in Canada. When the boys were eight months old, their parents took them to be circumcised. Unfortunately, this routine procedure had tragic results for one of the babies. Doctors used an unconventional method of circumcision and little Bruce Reimer's penis was burned off accidentally. His parents were horrified, but the doctors had an answer. Believing that gender differences were only environmental, they advised Bruce's parents to buy him dresses and dolls and to raise him as a girl. Bruce became Brenda. Later on, his genitals were surgically altered to resemble a girl's, and "she" was taken to psychiatrists to help her form a female identity.

Brenda was not fooled, however. She didn't want to wear dresses or play with the girls. She wanted boys' toys and to play with her brother and his friends. When she did play with the other girls, Brenda was bossy and demanding, and she wanted everyone to play rowdy, active games. She struggled in school; although her twin brother passed easily from grade to grade, Brenda was held back because her social and emotional skills were found lacking.

Brenda received estrogen injections as a teenager but was never attracted to boys. She was physically awkward, did not look feminine, and was teased and excluded by the other girls. She became so depressed that she began to consider suicide.

Finally, when Brenda was fourteen, her father told her the truth about her birth. In interviews (and in John Colapinto's account of Bruce/Brenda's story, *As Nature Made Him: The Boy Who Was Raised as a Girl)*, Bruce reports that the news came as a relief. Finally, what he'd been feeling all his life made sense. Bruce eventually received male hormone injections and had surgical reconstruction; he changed his name to David and married at the age of twenty-five, saying that he felt happy as a man. Unfortunately, David and his wife eventually separated, his twin brother died, and David committed suicide at the age of thirty-eight. If gender goes deeper than physical appearance—and, as David Reimer's story certainly shows, it does—you may be wondering what it really means to be male.

Research about Boys and Girls

In most ways, girls and boys are very much alike. Both boys and girls need love, belonging, and encouragement. They need character, life skills, and patience. Boys and girls need kind, firm discipline, and connection with parents and caring adults. Male and female brains are far more alike than different throughout most of the human life span. Still, there are some gender-related differences that appear to be a part of our children at birth.

Alert!

While male children are often slower to develop speech, language, and emotional skills than are girls, don't overlook differences in your son's development that may mean he needs extra help. A parent's instincts are usually worth trusting. If you believe your son needs extra attention, do not hesitate to check with your pediatrician or other specialists for evaluation and support.

Babies are exposed to sex hormones in the womb, and this appears to cause male and female brains to grow in slightly different ways. In her fascinating study of gender, Susan Gilbert points out some surprising differences between boy and girl babies:

- Women often labor longer to give birth to male infants than female infants.
- Male infants appear to be more easily stressed than female infants.
- Girls are often able to maintain eye contact sooner than boys,

and they are more social earlier in their infancy.

- Boys are often fussier babies; they cry more easily and have a harder time calming themselves down than do girls.
- Boys appear to be more emotionally vulnerable than girls; they have more difficulty responding to changes in routine and to parental anger and depression.
- Girls usually develop fine motor skills and language sooner than do boys.
- Boys are more impulsive and learn the skills related to self-control more slowly than do girls.
- Boys are more physically active and choose competitive play ("Bet you can't do this as good as me!") far more often than girls do.

Of course, these differences are generalizations, and your son is a unique individual, not exactly like any other child. As the years pass (always more quickly than you expect), you will come to know the special and fascinating young person your son is.

Who's Easier?

It is difficult to answer the age-old question of whether girls or boys are easier to raise. To explore the dynamics of this question, imagine a group of women getting together for a playdate with their young children. One mother expresses to her two friends that lately she is exhausted. Her son still wakes up several times a night, and he's fussy and irritable. She thought boys were supposed to be tough, but her son hates change, and once he starts crying, it's hard to calm him down. He hangs onto her leg and wails. Sometimes she wants to go hide under the bed! She looks at her friend who has a daughter the same age as her son and expresses her envy because raising a girl seems so easy. She is beginning to think a girl would have been a lot simpler to raise than her boy.

Their other friend, also the mother of a son, mentions that her son is just as mellow as her friend's daughter. He's happy to sit with a magazine and look at the pictures, although he loves to kick a soccer ball with his dad. This mother doesn't think she would have the patience for all the dresses and shoes and hair barrettes that come with raising a girl. Boys just get up and go, no muss and no fuss.

Essential

Sarah Johns, Ph.D., of Kent University found that optimistic women are more likely to have sons. She found that for every extra year a woman thought she would live, the odds of her firstborn being a boy increased. Research shows that women in good health and living in comfortable conditions also have a tendency to give birth to boys.

It's an old debate: Who is easier to raise, boys or girls? And the definitive answer is: It depends. As you've learned, boys can be more physically and emotionally sensitive during their early years, while girls seem to acquire language and social skills more quickly. Many parents believe girls are more demanding during adolescence than boys are. Still, each child is a complex and unique individual, and there are no one-size-fits-all rules about gender.

Stella Chess, M.D., and Alexander Thomas, M.D., have spent years studying temperament and the miracle of human personality. You will learn more about temperament in Chapter 4, but it may interest you to know that there is such a thing as goodness of fit. Simply put, you have a temperament, and so does your son. Sometimes, parents and their children mesh easily, working together smoothly to connect, grow, and solve problems. Other times, however, the process isn't so smooth.

Parental needs and expectations can complicate the process of raising a son. What happens if you are an active, athletic adult and you find yourself raising a quiet, dreamy little boy? What if you cherish art, music, and dance and find yourself with a boy who lives to play video games? Or you may be committed to peace and the environment and discover that your beloved son insists on building weapons out of LEGOs and firing away at anything that moves. Even loving and committed parents can feel disappointment that their children don't share their interests or fit their definition of an ideal boy. But that disappointment can create problems of its own, for you and for your son.

 **Fact**

Technology such as MRIs and PET scans have enabled researchers to look within living human brains. Their discoveries form the basis for the modern understanding of how boys and girls differ, especially early in life. Politically correct or not, the human brain is a highly sexualized organ and has a significant impact on determining the nature of girls and boys.

Myths about Raising Boys

Imagine the movie heroes of your own youth, facing an onslaught of enemies single-handed, rescuing the fair damsel, and saving the world in the process. (Until quite recently, action heroes could only be male!) Shouldn't every little boy want to be John Wayne or Bruce Willis? Will a son be tied to the apron strings or become a mama's boy if he enjoys a close relationship with his mother? Should fathers have the final say in parenting their sons? Shouldn't a healthy boy be at least part Huckleberry Finn?

The Power of Stereotypes

You may believe you are not influenced by cultural stereotypes about gender, but assumptions about boys, girls, and what makes them who they are run deep throughout literature, entertainment, and culture. For instance, in 2004, female golfer Annika Sorenstam was invited to play in a PGA Tour men's tournament. A number of male golfers were quite vocal in their opinion that she belonged on her own tour. One golfer went so far as to say he would not play with her and hoped she played badly.

 Essential

Sometimes parents touch, cuddle, and speak to infant boys less often than girls in an unconscious effort to make them stronger. Always remember that your son needs your affection, your tenderness, and lots of face-to-face conversation and play. You can teach skills, self-reliance, and confidence and still enjoy lots of healthy hugs and cuddles with your little boy.

The 2005 Indianapolis 500 automobile race was fascinating because not only was there a female driver, Danica Patrick, but because she drove well and led the race several times, much to the consternation of some of the male drivers and crews. One disgruntled crew member said to the press that Patrick should "wear white so she'd look like the other domestic appliances."

Boys Will Be Boys?

Gender assumptions work the other way around as well. The popular movie *Meet the Parents* had lots of fun with the notion that the hero, played by Ben Stiller, was a male nurse. And given a choice, many fathers would rather that their sons develop a love for football than a fondness for playing the flute. The soft-spoken, gentle young man who cares about appearance and loves the arts has become synonymous with homosexuality. In fact, among today's adolescents, "gay" is a word used to describe anything that is weird, dorky, or appalling. Boys, it turns out, had better be *boys* (or risk being teased and harassed).

What Is a Typical Boy?

Take a moment to think: Suppose someone asked you to describe a typical boy. What would you say? You might describe a rough-and-tumble boy who loves to run and climb, to play baseball or soccer, and to get dirty building fortresses in the backyard. You might describe a young person who is courteous, respectful, kind, reliable, strong, and able to take care of himself—well, at least most of the time. You might talk about a boy with holes in the knees of his jeans, untied shoelaces, and a face smeared with jelly, one with worms in his pockets and a reluctance to show weakness. Perhaps your typical boy would be stoic and strong, courageous in the face of danger, and fearless when faced with a challenge.

But is that an accurate description of a real boy? More importantly, is it an accurate description of your own son? Sometimes flesh-and-blood boys don't match their parents' expectations, with consequences that are troubling for everyone.

Exploring Your Own Expectations

As you will learn in the chapters ahead, what you believe about boys in general and your own son in particular will have a powerful influence on the child, the young man, and the adult your son becomes. As his parent, you shape the world your son inhabits, teaching him by your example as well as your words about the things that truly matter in life. You will teach him—often without realizing you are doing so—about men, women, love, life, and success. Your son will begin his life by seeing himself through your eyes. If you're thinking that this is a heavy responsibility, you're correct.

There is a story that star football quarterback Vinny Testaverde's father placed a football in his crib on the day he was born. Throughout his childhood and adolescence, Vinny lived with the idea that his destiny in life was to be a great football player. And he succeeded. But what if Vinny had not liked football? What if he played only to please his father, fearing the loss of his dad's love and approval if he quit the game?

Question?

What if I want very much for my son to follow in my footsteps, but he refuses?
People prefer an invitation to a command. You can teach your son about what you enjoy and share it with him, but you cannot force him to become something he is not. He will be healthiest and happiest when he is free to explore his own path—with your guidance and support.

All parents have hopes and dreams for their children; you will, too. But part of being a wise and loving parent is balancing your own expectations for your son with a realistic understanding of who your son truly is, the boy he is at heart and soul.

Think for a moment about your own childhood. What was the mood in the home you grew up in? Did you feel good enough just as you were, or were your parents critical and demanding? What do you think your parents believed about your siblings? Were you loved more, or less? Did you feel a sense of belonging and worth, or did you constantly have to work harder to earn your parents' approval? What impact do you think your childhood has had on your adult life?

All children are born hardwired to connect to their parents. And all children crave their parents' love, approval, and support. As the years pass, you will undoubtedly discover that your son's task in life is to become himself. He will match your expectations in some ways and surprise you in many others.

What Do You Want for Your Son?

Imagine for a moment that someone has handed you the keys to a beautiful, high-powered new car. Let's say that you don't check the tires, the gas, or the oil. You don't decide on a destination or get out a map. You don't pack a lunch or water to drink. You just jump behind the wheel, turn the ignition, and stomp on the accelerator. What do you suppose will happen?

Sometimes parents approach raising a child just that impulsively. Each day becomes its own crisis; you must get your son to sleep through the night, crawl, walk, use the toilet, and eventually, go off to school. He must learn to do his homework and his chores, drive, and come home on time. It can be tempting to look no farther ahead than today's challenges, and there will certainly be many of those as you parent your growing boy. Short-range parenting may work for today, but it may not be the best approach for your son's long-range health and happiness—or yours.

Long-Range Parenting

Here's a suggestion: Imagine that thirty years have gone by and your son is now an adult. What sort of life do you want him to have? What character qualities are important to you? When he is grown, what kind of man do you want him to be? Take the time to sit down with your son's other parent, or on your own if you are single, and write down the answers to these questions. Most parents discover that they have never really thought about parenting in this way before.

You may find that you want your son to be responsible, compassionate, confident, and kind. You may want him to be successful, educated, spiritual, and independent. You may wish for him stable relationships, a happy marriage, and healthy children of his own someday. The sobering truth about raising a son is that you are the one who must build these qualities into your son. Every day of your lives together, each challenge that you face and each problem that you solve is an opportunity to *teach* character, skills, and attitudes.

Roots and Wings

Write down your list and post it where you will see it often. Then, as each day with your son goes by, use your list as a map to your final destination. The spilled juice, the temper tantrum, and the homework left undone—all are opportunities to teach your son what he needs to know to be successful and happy and to build a relationship that will last both of you a lifetime.

A wise person once said that a parent's job is to give a child both roots and wings—roots so they always know that they can return home for love and comfort and wings so they can soar. Learning to know the fascinating person your boy really is will help you give him the foundation and the joy he needs to soar through life.

CHAPTER 2

Preparing Yourself to Raise Your Son

For generations, experts have debated variations on an old question: Is it nature or nurture? Are genes and heredity most important in raising a child, or is it environment? What really determines who a child will become? The answer is both—but much more than both. Your son's journey toward adulthood is influenced by the traits and qualities he was born with, but it is also shaped by who you are, and what you bring to the act of parenting.

How Parents Affect Their Children

How do we become who we are? Well, here's a simple explanation. A child is born with a certain set of traits and genetic tendencies. He may be short or tall, blond or dark-haired; he may have physical strength and coordination or an inborn gift for music and creativity. He may be optimistic or naturally negative. This child, like all children, has parents. Perhaps he has a loving father and mother and lives in a comfortable home. Perhaps he has a single mother, or is put up for adoption at birth. He will have to use the abilities he was born with to make sense of his surroundings, and to decide how to thrive—or how to survive.

 **Fact**

The decisions and experiences you encountered growing up have shaped the way your brain responds to relationships—including your relationship with your son. Exploring and understanding your childhood experiences will help you understand and connect with your son as he grows.

One of the traits that makes us human is our need to attach meaning to everything we experience. We create meaning—in other words, we make unconscious decisions—about everything in our lives, from whether or not we're loved and wanted to whether we're smart, or cute, or athletic. Researchers call these early decisions adaptations and say that much of adult personality consists of the adaptations we've formed along our life's journey. Not surprisingly, parents have a significant impact on the adaptations their children make.

You will undoubtedly discover as you raise your son that parenthood invites you to come to terms with your own early life. One of the most valuable things you can do as a parent is to spend time understanding your own experiences and what you have decided about yourself and others as a result. Daniel J. Siegel, M.D., and Mary Hartzell, M.Ed., suggest some questions to ponder in their thought-provoking look at neurobiology and parenting, *Parenting from the Inside Out*. Take a moment to think about these questions and write down your answers:

- Who was in your family when you were growing up?
- What was your relationship with your mother like? Your father? Do you ever try to be like (or different from) one of your parents?
- How did your parents discipline you? How do you feel that affects your role as a parent now?

- How did your parents communicate with you when you were happy and excited? When you were angry or unhappy, what would happen? Did your father and mother respond differently to you during emotional times? How?
- What impact do you think your childhood has had on your adult life in general, including the way you think of yourself as a parent and the way you relate to your own children? If you could change something about the way you relate to your son, what would it be?

You may not think your own experiences have anything to do with how you raise your son, but the fascinating field of attachment research teaches us otherwise. Parents who have come to terms with their own past—who have what is called a coherent narrative of their childhood and early life—are better prepared to have healthy relationships with their own children.

Learning from Your Parents

Your answer to the questions about your childhood probably stirred up some old memories. Perhaps some were happy; others may have made you feel sad or even angry. Take the time to reflect on your memories and notice whether or not it's easy to tell your own story. If you can start at the beginning of your life and relate your autobiography smoothly, without large gaps, and without feelings of trauma or distress, chances are that you have a coherent narrative.

Stories—our own and those of others—are how we make sense of our lives. Researchers tell us that what happens to us is not as important as what we *decide* about what happens to us. In other words, the meaning you have attached to your early experiences is more important than the facts of what happened to you.

Your parents shaped your early experiences, for better or worse. You are now shaping your son's. Taking the time to understand where you came from (and decide where you want to go) will help you be a wise and caring parent.

The Nature of Attachment

Long ago, even experts believed that the human brain had a solitary existence within a single human skull. New technology, however, has allowed scientists to peer within the living brain, and what they have discovered is both exciting and sobering. Your brain is a highly social organ. It is designed to connect with other brains, and it literally changes its structure and function over your life span. The most powerful element in creating these changes is relationship, relationships with family, friends, or other significant people in your life.

 Essential

When children have a predictable and repeatable experience of being cared for, it creates what is called a secure base. Security gives children the sense of well-being necessary to explore their world and develop in healthy ways. Understanding yourself and offering a secure base to your son is vital in getting him off to a good start in life.

Secure Attachment

About half of all people have a secure attachment. This means that they have enjoyed responsive care and communication with a parent or other caregiver and have felt supported at times of emotional stress. Other people have not been so fortunate. Their parents were not able to offer them a secure attachment, and their ability to have strong, healthy relationships is affected.

As Daniel Siegel, M.D., and Mary Hartzell, M.Ed., point out in *Parenting from the Inside Out,* how you respond to your son's emotions is vital. Imagine that your excited little boy brings you a beetle. You might say, "Wow, look at how green his wings are! Thank you for showing him to me." Or you might say, "Get that thing out of the house right now!" Your responses over time will help determine how connected and understood your son feels with you.

The Power of Attachment

You may have had a secure attachment with your own parents and now find it easy to be perceptive, supportive, and responsive with your own son (at least most of the time). Research tells us, however, that when a parent is unwilling or unable to respond to a child consistently, the child will adapt by avoiding closeness to the parent, or by becoming anxious about the relationship.

 *Fact*

Children who were abused or neglected often fail to develop the ability to reason well, to regulate emotions, or to connect well with others. Attachment, it turns out, is a powerful predictor of the relationships we have later in life.

Parents who had an insecure attachment to their own parents are often emotionally unavailable, unresponsive, overly intrusive, or rejecting with their own children. They may lack empathy and find it difficult to deal with their children's emotions or to offer love and nurturing. The good news, however, is that attachment can change.

No child gets to choose his parents, and perhaps your early experiences did not teach you what you need to know to connect easily with your son. Understanding your own story, perhaps through counseling with a skilled therapist, can help a great deal and will provide you with the understanding and awareness you need to become the parent you hope to be.

Self-Care and Balance

Imagine a couple named Jim and Marilyn. They had tried and waited for almost nine years before their first child was born. When Willy finally arrived, Jim and Marilyn found themselves happily planning their entire lives around him.

Jim continued to work, but Marilyn left her job in real estate and became a stay-at-home mom. After all, they'd heard that child care is not good for young children. They stopped going to their dance class because Willy cried when the babysitter arrived, and they stopped going to church because Willy didn't do well in the nursery. Willy liked to be held; he cried when he was put down, so Marilyn always had him riding on one hip as she went about her chores during the day.

As Willy grew, he had every new toy, his own computer, and the most fashionable clothing. He went to gym class, swim class, soccer, tee-ball, and play groups every afternoon. Marilyn began to feel cranky and depressed; she was always in the car and missed working out and talking to her friends. Jim missed the lively, energetic partner he'd had before Willy's birth. Both parents remained devoted to their son, but both began to secretly wonder: Don't parents get to have a life, too?

Treat Yourself with Respect

Many parents believe that raising a healthy boy with good self-esteem means doing everything for him and giving him everything he wants. In fact, so many American parents believe this that marketers now spend $15 billion a year selling products to children and adolescents, two-and-a-half times the amount spent only a decade ago. Why? They know who actually controls the finances in most families: It's the children.

Your son deserves the best you can give him. He needs your time, energy, commitment, patience, and love. But take a moment to think: If you always put yourself last on your list of priorities, what will happen to your own physical and emotional health? What will your son decide about his place in the world? About you? The long-term results of always putting your son first may not be what you intend—or what you want.

Caring for Yourself

Remember, your son is watching you constantly for clues about what matters most in life. He will learn to respect you when you respect yourself; he will learn to value and appreciate life when you show him how. And he will learn to be demanding and self-centered if your actions teach him that he should always get what he wants the moment he wants it. Raising a healthy son requires that you be a healthy parent.

Keep Yourself Physically Healthy

Exercise is a powerful antidepressant and antianxiety remedy; it also strengthens your heart and mind. Take time on a regular basis to take a yoga class, work out, play a sport, or take a vigorous walk with a friend. Eat a healthy diet and do your best to get enough sleep. You will have more energy and patience (and less illness) if you take care of your body.

Keep Yourself Mentally Alert

More than one parent of a young child has found himself cutting a friend's meat at dinner or babbling about toilet training. Don't forget to be a grownup on occasion. You can take a class once a week, take time to read a good book, or enjoy other stimulating activities. You will tolerate the routines and repetition of parenting far better when you have something of your own to look forward to.

Keep Yourself Emotionally Connected

Much as you undoubtedly love your son, you are still an adult, and you need adult support and connection. Do your best to make time for friendship; a telephone call to a friend can help you through the most difficult moments of life with a little one. Get together with other parents of children your son's age and share stories and experiences. It helps a great deal to know you're not alone.

Keep Yourself Spiritually Strong

You may find strength and comfort in church, or you may nurture yourself spiritually with work for the environment or a cause you believe in. Whatever it is that you are passionate about, be sure you make time for it in your daily life. Your son will learn best from your example, and the values you cherish can be something you share for a lifetime.

Wisdom, Not Selfishness

You may believe it is selfish to do things for yourself when you are a parent, and it is true that spending time with your son and time as a family are important. But taking care of yourself is not selfishness; it is wisdom. Imagine that the energy you possess is like water in a crystal pitcher. Every time you do something for someone else, deal with a crisis, or make a decision, you pour water out of your pitcher. What will happen when the pitcher is empty? Finding ways to keep your own pitcher full—by taking time to be physically, mentally, and spiritually healthy—is one of the most important aspects of being a wise and loving parent.

A Word about Your Marriage

If you are a single parent, you face your own joys and challenges. If you are parenting with a partner, however, you need to take a moment to consider the impact of parenthood on your relationship. You might think that having a child would bring a couple closer together. After all, there is the joy of birth and the delight parents share in watching their youngster grow, learn, and explore his world. It isn't always easy, however.

John Gottman, Ph.D., of the University of Washington has spent years studying marriage. He has found that 40 to 70 percent of all couples experience stress, conflict, and a drop in marital satisfaction when a baby comes home.

Why? Well, moms often provide most of the hands-on care for infants, nursing the baby, walking the floor when he cries, and getting up several times during the night. A new mother may experience postpartum depression and may have little energy for fun with dad. Fathers, on the other hand, often report feeling excluded by the mother-and-baby duo and may find other ways of occupying themselves while their child is young. Sometimes the patterns that form during a child's early years are difficult to change as that child grows. When their son leaves home for good, what will remain of his parents' relationship?

Alert!

Researchers at Ohio State University have found that couples who had a good relationship with each other when their child was an infant, but who disagreed about parenting, were more likely to have a poor relationship by the time their child was three years old. How you and your partner decide to coparent your son influences your marriage.

Remember, children watch the people around them and make decisions about what it all means. What will your son decide as he watches your relationship with his other parent? Numerous studies have shown that the way parents resolve conflict, express affection, support each other, communicate, and handle their sexual relationship has a strong influence on their children.

Here's the news: All parents disagree, at least occasionally, about parenting. Most of the time, one parent tends to be strict while the other is more lenient. Then parents argue about who is right rather than working together to solve problems effectively. Unfortunately, parenting styles and beliefs rarely become obvious until *after* children arrive, making the challenges seem even more daunting.

Be sure to take time for your marriage, to have fun, and to connect with your partner. If you disagree about parenting, take a parenting class or read a good parenting book together, and then talk together about what you want to do for your son. Be sure there is time in every day for affection, laughter, and conversation. Your son will be watching and learning from what he sees.

What You Will Do as a Parent

Your son is an important factor in how your life together works. But as you are learning, you are vitally important, too. In fact, if you haven't already figured it out, the only person in your life whom you can ever control is yourself. Unfortunately, that doesn't stop many adults from trying to control their partners and their children. Change always begins with you.

The Value of Self-Control

When you lose your temper (or when your son loses his), the part of your brain responsible for thinking and reasoning disconnects, leaving you with only physical sensation and emotion. No one can solve problems effectively when he is angry. Before you respond to a challenge from your son, take a moment to calm yourself down. Then think about what you want your son to learn. A moment to breathe is always a good idea.

Imagine that it is a parent's carpool day. Michael is driving his nine-year-old son Caleb, Caleb's younger sister Valerie, and her best friend, Jessica, to school when an argument erupts in the back seat. "Dad," Caleb shouts, "Valerie took my pencil!" Michael has been through this routine before. He isn't about to drive a carload of shrieking children, so he pulls quietly over onto a side street.

"Hey," Caleb asks, "where are we? We're going to be late for school, Dad."

Michael looks at his son in the rearview mirror. "I guess you might," he said with a friendly smile. "But you know I can't drive when you're fighting in the car. You three let me know when you've worked it out, and we'll go on to school." Then Michael calmly picks up a magazine and begins reading.

There is a moment of stunned silence. Then Caleb looks at his sister. "We're going to be late," he says, "and I'm hall monitor today. Will you give me back the pencil? Please?"

"Come on, Valerie," Jessica says, looking worried. "I don't want to be late, either."

"Oh, all right," Valerie says, tossing the pencil into Caleb's lap. "There's your old pencil. Dad, can we go now?"

Michael looks up from his magazine. "Have you solved your problem?"

Three only slightly sulky faces nod back at him. "Good, then. Let's get going," he says, and they continue to school.

What You Decide Matters

Michael had learned the value of controlling his own words and behavior rather than attempting to control his children. Is it always this easy? Well, no. But thinking carefully about your own thoughts, feelings, and actions is an excellent place to begin in creating a strong, loving relationship with your son.

 *Question?*

What if my son doesn't do what I tell him to?
Tell him, for instance, "I will read when you are sitting quietly." Then sit quietly looking at the book. He may run, and then look to see what you are doing. If he wants a story, he will sit down. If he doesn't, close the book. He will learn that you mean what you say.

You are your son's earliest and best teacher. What you believe about yourself, what you've decided about your own experiences, and how you manage your own behavior will have a powerful impact on your growing boy.

CHAPTER 3

The Basics of Parenting Your Son

Walk into any bookstore and you can't help but notice the abundance of parenting books. Each year more books appear, filled with suggestions about how to raise your child. Celebrities, psychologists, your in-laws, your neighbors and friends—everyone these days is an expert, or so they claim. But here's the truth about parenting: You are the expert on your child. Learn all you can about what matters most; then trust your own wisdom and knowledge of your son.

Belonging and Significance

Most parents have lots and lots of questions. You may be wondering how to help your son sleep through the night, become toilet trained, or dress himself. You may have questions about chores, allowance, or homework. Or you may be wondering if organized sports are really a good idea, how much television your son should watch, or whether to allow him to play video games. You will learn more about these issues in the pages ahead, but long before you can address all the daily challenges of raising a boy, something very important has to happen. It's called a relationship.

Love Is Not Enough

You may believe that the most important gift you can give your growing son is love. But parents often do many ineffective or even hurtful things in the name of love. For instance, one parent may say, "I give my kids everything they want because I love them." Another says, "I make my kids work hard for everything because I love them and it's a tough world out there." Parents criticize their children, punish their children, and pamper their children, all in the name of love.

Love is rarely the real problem in parenting. If you've ever watched your child sleep at night, you know how overwhelming that sense of heartfelt love can be. But love is most effective when it is blended with understanding, wisdom, and the ability to think about the long-term results of your decisions. Fortunately, research and experience are giving us new information almost every day about how best to raise healthy, capable children.

Pioneers in Parenting

Alfred Adler, M.D., and Rudolf Dreikurs, M.D., were among the pioneers in studying and understanding children's behavior. Dr. Adler was a psychiatrist who lived in Vienna around the time of Freud, but who disagreed with his better-known colleague about almost everything. Dr. Dreikurs, also a Viennese psychiatrist, built his work on the teachings of Adler and eventually moved to the United States, where in the 1930s he introduced the idea of parenting education to American audiences. Dr. Dreikurs advocated relationships built on mutual respect and recognized that more than love alone, children need a sense of belonging and significance in their families.

Why Belonging and Significance Matter

Children learn about life in the context of relationships, and their earliest relationships are the most important. Regardless of their gender, appearance, or talents, all children need to know that they *belong*, that there is a place in their families just for them. Children need to know that they are accepted unconditionally and wanted in spite of their occasionally difficult behavior. Sounds easy, doesn't it? But ask any parent of a cranky, defiant three-year-old and she will tell you that it isn't always as easy as it sounds.

Children also need to have a sense of their own significance, the knowledge that they have worth apart from what they do or achieve and that the choices they make in life matter. In fact, Dr. Adler believed that all humans have an inborn desire to connect with the community around them and to give something back. In the aftermath of the September 11, 2001, terrorist attacks in New York City, children all over the country sold lemonade, collected coins, and made contributions to help the children of New York. In many cases, no one told them to; they just wanted to do something helpful. That is belonging and significance at work. Children who know they belong and that they matter in their families and their world are more likely to become capable, productive members of their communities.

Fact

Alfred Adler, M.D., believed in treating children respectfully, but he also believed that pampering and spoiling were discouraging and eventually led to social and behavioral problems. Dr. Adler's ideas are the foundation of democratic teaching and parenting approaches, which are now widely recognized as being most effective in promoting healthy brain development and strong relationships.

Why Relationship Matters to Boys

Several years ago, a group of doctors, psychologists, and other researchers began studying a troubling problem. The rates of both behavioral and emotional problems among American children and adolescents appeared to be rising, and no one could really explain why. After all, our material wealth and comforts were improving. Why would children be suffering more?

Many observers of American life in the twenty-first century have noticed that the pace of family life appears to be accelerating at an alarming rate. It is now common for both mothers and fathers to work outside the home and for children to spend a large part of their early lives in child care. Even when the family is at home together, there seems to be little time for real connection. Everyone has his own television, computer, and cell phone. There are household chores to do. Work follows parents home, while children have outside activities and piles of homework. Multitasking is fine, unless parenting becomes just another task on the list of things to do.

Alert!

More than 8 percent of U.S. high school students suffer from clinical depression; U.S. children as a group report more anxiety today than did psychiatric patients in the 1950s; and about 21 percent of U.S. children ages nine to seventeen have a diagnosable mental or addictive disorder. These problems can stem from a lack of connection to significant adults.

There are many ways to help children develop a healthy sense of belonging and significance. Among them are encouragement, listening, spending time together, effective and respectful discipline, and the teaching of character and life skills. For a moment, though, let's go all the way back to the beginning and take a look at the earliest moments of life with your boy.

Connecting with Your Son

Researchers now say that the human brain is hardwired from birth for one specific task: to connect with other brains. If you're the parent of a baby boy, that means *you*. Allan N. Schore, Ph.D., of the David Geffen School of Medicine at UCLA, puts it this way, "The idea is that we are born to form attachments, that our brains are physically wired to develop in tandem with another's, through emotional communication, beginning before words are spoken."

Simply put, your baby boy needs connection with you as much as he needs food, safety, and shelter. When you hold him, rock him, and gaze into his eyes, you are helping his brain develop the circuitry for relationship and future learning. You may recall that infant boys may actually be more emotionally and physically fragile than infant girls. Your son needs lots of tenderness, time, and attention from you to develop and grow.

Creating Contingency

Consider for a moment a familiar scenario. It's late afternoon; your baby has been taking his nap and is still in his crib. You are in the kitchen, getting ready for dinner and the evening ahead of you. Suddenly, you hear your baby crying. What do you do? Well, most parents instinctively head for the bedroom to find out what's going on. Perhaps your baby just woke up and is eager to be picked up and cuddled. Perhaps he's hungry or wet. He may even have developed a fever while he was sleeping and be feeling miserable.

Your own parental instincts kick in when you hold and look at your baby, and while all parents get their signals crossed occasionally, most of the time you know just what to do. Attentive parents and their babies enjoy what researchers call contingent communication, and as it turns out, contingent communication may be the most important single building block in brain development and relationship, as well as one of the few parenting skills that occurs in all known cultures.

Suppose that something gets in the way of this process. Perhaps the television is on and you don't hear the baby crying at all. Or you're depressed and tired and just don't feel like walking all the way back to your son's room to see what's wrong. Maybe you think he's hungry when he's actually wet, or you miss the fact that he has a fever or a rash. In this case, the baby's needs will not be met. This is not contingent communication. No parent is perfect; no matter how hard you try, you will get the message wrong from time to time. But as long as your son learns that you listen, you care, and you will respond to his needs the best you can, he will grow and thrive.

Fact

Contingent communication means that a child's signal is received and understood and that a parent responds appropriately. When communication between parent and child is caring and connected, a child thrives and his relationship with his parents grows stronger. Listening and responding to your son are two of the most important things you can do for him.

Because boys usually lag behind girls in the development of their emotional and social skills, it is vital that you take time to listen, touch, talk, and connect with your son. He needs relationship with you in order to become a happy, productive young man.

What about Birth Order?

There are many ways of understanding your son and his place in his world. One of those is birth order, or the way the pieces of your family fit together. There's an old saying that every child is born into a different family, and if you think about it for a moment, you can see how true that is. Firstborn children live in a world populated by adults, while youngest children have to share their busy parents with a sibling or two from the moment they arrive. Birth order is not a good way to predict a child's behavior or personality, but it can be a useful way of understanding that child's perceptions about himself and you.

Firstborn Children

Not surprisingly, firstborn children receive a huge amount of parental attention. They are the first arrivals into a new family and usually have the most privileges—and more responsibilities than their siblings as they grow up. (In some cultures, firstborn sons are treated like princes and receive a great deal of special treatment.) Not surprisingly, firstborns usually learn language more quickly than their later siblings, since they have adults talking to them all the time. Many firstborns learn that the way to get love and belonging is to please parents; they may become perfectionists and high achievers. Sometimes, though, they feel so overwhelmed by the pressure placed on them that they drop out and quit trying.

Only Children

Only children are firstborns but more so. They are often comfortable being alone and entertaining themselves, but they may struggle a bit with social skills such as sharing and cooperation with friends. Wise parents will help an only child enter the world of his peers and offer lots of opportunities to play, share, and practice getting along.

Youngest Children

These are the "babies" of the family. They are often charming and friendly, and they may be quite skilled at getting others to take care of them. (Their older siblings usually think they're spoiled.) Sometimes parents have relaxed both their rules and their expectations by the time the youngest child comes along, and the youngest may try to rush the process of gaining privileges enjoyed by his older siblings.

Middle Children

You may have heard someone say, "Oh, he's a middle child," as if that explains everything. Truthfully, middle children are often in a tight spot. They don't have the privileges of the oldest, nor do they get the attention of the youngest. Middle children may look for special ways to define themselves and be noticed, choosing activities that siblings aren't interested in, for example, or resisting parental expectations. They often focus on peers more than adults and are sometimes seen as rebels in their families.

Remember, all children need a sense of belonging and significance, and all children need connection. Birth order is only one way to understand how your son perceives his place in your family and his own importance in his world.

Essential

Think about your own childhood when examining birth order. Were you a firstborn? A youngest child? How did your position in your family influence your sense of belonging and significance? How do you think your siblings, if you had any, felt about your family? How might your son's birth order affect his beliefs about himself?

Understanding the Beliefs Behind Behavior

Parents spend a great deal of time, energy, and resources attempting to shape and change their child's behavior. Many approaches to discipline, such as punishment, rewards, time-out, grounding, or taking away possessions and privileges, are attempts to control what a child does.

There is a more effective way, however. Children want connection; they need a sense of belonging and significance. But being children, young and unskilled, they do not always understand how to go about getting what they need in positive ways. So they do whatever seems to work, and when you're a young child that can mean just about anything.

Beliefs Behind Behavior in Action

To better understand the importance of uncovering the beliefs behind your son's behavior, imagine the following scenario. Kim is a busy mom. She runs a business from her home and often must spend a great deal of time on the telephone. This is fine with Kim, but it does not always work out well for Timothy, her four-year-old son. Like all little boys his age, Timothy wants a sense of belonging and connection with his mom, and when you're four years old and an only child, that means her undivided attention.

One morning the phone rings, and Kim settles down with a notepad to talk to her client. Timothy, who has been happily building a castle with his blocks, looks over at her and sighs. You can almost hear him thinking, "Not again." But Timothy knows just how to get his mother's attention.

"Moo-o-m," he whines, tugging on Kim's jeans. "I need some juice."

"Sshhh, honey, I'm on the phone," Kim whispers, and then says into the phone, "hold on a moment, it's my little boy." "You know where the juice boxes are, Timothy," Kim says impatiently. "Go ahead and get yourself one."

Kim returns to her call, and Timothy wanders into the kitchen. He gets himself a juice box from the refrigerator but—uh-oh—manages to spill half of it putting the straw in the little hole. When his mom sees the mess, Timothy gives her a "who me?" look, puts the box down in the puddle of juice, and begins to draw designs on the kitchen floor in fruit punch.

 **Fact**

Jane Nelsen, Ed.D., points out that children's behavior is a form of code. Their actions are their way of telling you what they think, feel, and need. Sometimes their behavior is misguided, but you will be a more effective parent when you look for the beliefs behind your child's behavior and work with him to solve the problems you face.

"Timothy, get a sponge," Kim says, but the damage is done. If she remains on the phone, Timothy will continue to invent new ways to attract her attention. He isn't really misbehaving intentionally, despite how it appears. He has just learned during his four years with Mom that misbehavior will get her attention even when good behavior does not. And having Mom mad at him feels more like connection to a four-year-old than being ignored.

Dealing with Beliefs Before Behavior

What should Kim do now? As you will learn in the chapters ahead, misbehavior is an invitation to look for solutions. Timothy seems to believe that he matters to his mom only when he has her undivided attention, and Kim will be most effective when she plans for these discouraging moments.

Yelling, lecturing, or sending Timothy to a punitive time-out are unlikely to help. After spending an hour with her favorite parenting book, Kim makes a plan.

1. **Kim sits down with Timothy and lets him know that she needs to spend some time on the phone for her business.** She reminds him that her business allows her to be at home with him, which is important to her, and she asks for his help. (Children can be cooperative and creative when asked for their ideas, or they can be defiant when ordered to obey.)

2. **Kim asks Timothy if he has any ideas about what he could do when she has to make a phone call.** Timothy ponders the question thoughtfully, and then suggests that they make a "phone bag" like the one they use for car trips. Kim agrees, and together they put together a bag of inexpensive small toys, books, and story tapes to be used only when Mom is on the phone.

3. **Kim decides to set some limits on when her clients can call her, and to let them know her office hours.** She realizes that creating a better balance between work and family time will help Timothy feel secure. She and Timothy also decide on a half-hour period every day that will become their special time, time when they can connect, talk, and play together.

4. **Kim and Timothy also agree to create a snack drawer, where Timothy can help himself to healthy snacks when his mom is too busy to get them for him.** Once the drawer is empty, though, there will be no more snacks for the day. Choosing when to eat them is up to Timothy. He quickly figures out that when his mom says no more snacks, she means no more snacks, and he learns to make them last.

5. **Kim and Timothy also use a kitchen timer to help Timothy learn to be patient.** When Kim makes a call, she sets the timer for the amount of time she believes she will be on the phone. Timothy gets to hold the timer; when it beeps, he can remind his mom to end her call and spend some time with him.

Will these ideas keep Timothy from whining and begging for his mother's attention? Well, perhaps for a while. These ideas deal with the beliefs and feelings *behind* Timothy's behavior and will help him learn to cooperate with his mom, but Kim and Timothy will need to have many such conversations in the years ahead. Looking for the beliefs behind your son's behavior will help you be a calmer, more effective parent.

Kindness and Firmness

Many parents are good at being either kind or firm. They are firm (strict, nagging, controlling, and punitive) in the belief that children need discipline and will become spoiled brats without it. Or they are "nice" to their children, failing to follow through with promised consequences, rescuing their children from their own mistakes, and offering lots of treats and goodies along the way in the belief that this will create happy children with good self-esteem. Unfortunately, neither parenting extreme is truly effective.

Toughening Up the Boys

Sadly, researchers have found that parents and teachers often are far harsher with boys than with girls, usually in an unspoken desire to toughen them up. As Dan Kindlon, Ph.D., and Michael Thompson, Ph.D., put it in *Raising Cain: Protecting the Emotional Life of Boys*, "Harsh discipline is presumed to help make a man out of a boy: he needs tough treatment to whip him into shape. The assumption is that boys are impervious to subtle suggestion and more resistant to abuse. This gender split reflects our underlying cultural belief that boys are made of 'different stuff' than girls. When it comes to their capacity for hurt and anger, this assumption is not true."

Alert!

Even loving parents need to pay attention to the way they discipline sons. One survey found that "normal" parents were just as likely to use physical punishment (spanking, smacking, yanking) as abusive parents when boys ran into the street, broke something valuable, or acted impulsively—things boys are far more likely to do than girls.

Kindness and Firmness at the Same Time

Dr. Dreikurs was the first to teach parents to practice being kind and firm at the same time. According to Jane Nelsen, Ed.D., Lynn Lott, M.A., and H. Stephen Glenn, Ph.D., in *Positive Discipline A–Z: 1001 Solutions to Everyday Parenting Problems*, "Firmness means using appropriate parenting principles with confidence. Kindness means maintaining dignity and respect for yourself and your child while using those parenting principles." In other words, kindness shows respect for the humanity of your son, while firmness shows respect for yourself and the requirements of the situation.

It takes practice to learn to be kind and firm at the same time; most parents are used to swinging from one to the other like an out-of-control pendulum. Being kind and firm *at the same time* truly is a magic key in raising your son, and it invites him to respect limits (and you) while feeling loved and secure.

Learning to Listen

Most parents are really good at talking. In fact, most parents do lots and lots of talking and wonder why no one seems to be listening. The old Charlie Brown cartoons delighted generations of children (and adults) when they showed the characters going about their business while the parents and teachers went "waaah, waaah, waaah" somewhere off-screen. Is that really how parents sound to children? Unfortunately, sometimes it is.

Listening to your son—really listening—is one of the most encouraging things you can do for him, and one of the best ways to build a sense of belonging and connection. Listening with your full attention (not just "hearing" him while you make dinner or drive the car) tells him that he matters to you and that you want to know what he is thinking, feeling, and deciding to do.

Think about someone you enjoy talking to. What does that person do that allows you to feel understood and cared about? Chances are he looks at you, offers you encouraging feedback, and doesn't glance at his watch every thirty seconds.

Many of the messages we send to those we love are nonverbal. That is, they are sent without words, in our facial expression, tone of voice, gestures, pauses, and body posture. Young children are especially sensitive to these messages and almost always can sense what you are really feeling.

Essential

Many messages your son sends you have no words; they are expressed in his actions and gestures. Be sure to make eye contact when you speak to your son and to watch him when he speaks to you. Actions truly do speak louder than words when you're raising a boy; be sure you tune in to your son's nonverbal messages.

Throughout your son's growing-up years, your ability to really listen to him will be one of your most valuable parenting skills. Here are some suggestions:

- **Make time in your day to listen.** It's fine to have conversations in the car or in the grocery store, but real listening takes time and focus. Being too busy to listen may keep you from ever really understanding your boy.
- **Listen patiently.** Many parents take the first opportunity to jump in with suggestions, solutions, or lectures, and then wonder why their sons say, "You never listen to me!" You will know best how to help your son if you listen calmly to what he has to say. You might even ask, "Is there anything more you want to tell me?" before responding.
- **Be sure you make eye contact.** If your son is physically smaller than you are, sit down next to him or find a way to get on the same level. (It's difficult to have a comfortable conversation with someone who towers over you!) Pay attention to your own nonverbal messages: Are you smiling? Glaring? Anxious to be somewhere else?
- **Be curious.** You may not share all of your son's interests or even approve of them. But the first step to solving problems is understanding, and understanding begins with listening. Invite your son to share his ideas, his joys, and his challenges with you, and take time to be genuinely curious rather than judgmental.

Listening is one of the best ways to enter your son's world and to get to know the young man he is becoming. You will always have a better idea of how to respond to your growing boy when you have taken the time to listen first.

The Message of Love

You will make many decisions during the years you are raising your son. Some of them will be easy; others will be difficult for both of you. You may believe that whatever you do, you are doing because you love your son. But does he know that?

A high school counselor sat with a group of students one day and asked them whether their parents loved them. The answers he received surprised him. "My parents love me when I get straight As," one boy responded. "Mine love me when I stay out of trouble," another responded. "I got caught drinking a couple of weeks ago, and boy, were they mad. They didn't talk to me for days." As the conversation continued, the counselor realized that many of the students believed their parents loved them only when they lived up to expectations, behaved appropriately, or achieved certain goals. Belonging and significance are unconditional, but these young people did not feel unconditionally loved.

As the years go by, you will undoubtedly have some tough moments with your son. Setting limits, following through, and deciding what values to teach are difficult challenges for all parents, and conflict with your son is inevitable. You will learn to be kind and firm, and to follow through when necessary because you know it is best for the boy you love. But what will *he* think, feel, and decide about you, about himself, and about the world he lives in? It may not be what you think.

Be sure you take time every day to ask yourself if the message of love—unconditional belonging and significance—is getting through to your boy. You may not always like his behavior or his attitude. There may be moments of heartache for both of you. You and your son can survive these challenges when you both know why you care. Wise parenting requires skill, but it must always be powered by love.

CHAPTER 4

Your Son's First Year

T he thinking and planning are done, the room is decorated, and the tiny outfits and supplies are ready. At last the day has come: You and your little boy are beginning your lives together. You probably know by now that the first few years of your son's life are critically important in his development; they will also set the tone for your relationship in the years ahead. What do you need to know as you begin this first important year of life together?

Physical Development and Parenting

Human infants are among the most helpless creatures alive. When they are born, babies cannot pick up their own heads, turn over, or move on their own. In fact, it takes a surprising amount of time for a baby to learn that those fluttery things in front of his face are his own hands and that those hands can be used to grasp and hold objects. In the beginning, your baby will sleep most of every day. (Nights may be another matter, unfortunately!)

Life with Baby

Can you remember the first time you saw your son's face? No matter how red and wrinkled he appeared, you undoubtedly fell in love at first sight. You may have dreamed of these early days and weeks together. Sometimes, though, the dreams fade a bit in the presence of reality. Your baby may cry endlessly, sleep when you're awake, wake up when you're longing for sleep, and dirty his diaper or burp up his

breakfast at the most inopportune moments. You may find yourself sifting through the piles of shower and baby gifts, wondering what a receiving blanket is for and which end of the onesie to put on first.

A good pediatrician is a must in these early months; be sure you feel comfortable asking your doctor questions because you will have lots of them. It can also be helpful to have family and friends who have raised children before and who can be your "consultants."

 **Fact**

A rule of thumb about physical development is that babies grow from the inside out and from the top down. The first parts to be fully developed are your son's heart and lungs; the last skill he acquires is fine motor control. He will be able to pick up and move his head before coordinating his arms and legs.

No one is born knowing how to be a parent; learn all you can and don't hesitate to ask for help. As a general rule, the first few months of life with your baby boy are *not* a good time to worry about keeping your house spotless, entertaining your gourmet club, or landscaping your yard. Keep your life as simple as possible. Your baby will need a great deal of your time and attention, and you should make sleep and caring for yourself a priority.

Parenting in the First Months of Life

Infants are not little adults; they are astonishingly resilient and are born wired to grow and learn, but they are not able to reason, remember, or practice self-control the way you can. Never leave your baby unattended, unless he is in his crib, infant seat, or other secure place. Many parents have had the unsettling experience of leaving a baby on a sofa or bed for "just a minute" and returning to discover that their baby chose just that moment to turn over for the first time—right onto the floor.

Even the happiest baby will do a fair amount of crying. Not surprisingly—crying is a baby's only form of communication. He will cry when he is tired, lonely, hungry, thirsty, too hot, or too cold. Sometimes he will cry just to soothe himself when he's overwhelmed with stimulation. (Remember, boys tend to cry more frequently and can be harder to soothe than girls.) With time and practice, you will learn to decipher your son's cries and will be able to give him just what he needs.

 **Essential**

You must decide whether to feed your son on demand or on a schedule, whether to let him sleep with you or only in his own crib, and whether or not to pick him up every time he cries. Whatever you decide, do it with confidence. If you are relaxed and calm, your baby is more likely to be relaxed.

It may seem in these first few months that everything in your life revolves around your baby, and in fact, it's probably true. By the time an infant is three months old or so, however, he usually will have settled and will have a more predictable routine. There are many resources available to help you decide about feeding, sleep habits, and physical care. No matter how overwhelmed you may occasionally feel, don't forget to take time to enjoy your son. These early months will be gone before you know it.

Brain Development

Not too long ago, even the experts believed that when a baby was born, his brain was more or less complete, and parents could focus on supplying skills and information. You may be surprised to learn, however, that your baby's brain will continue to grow within his skull for quite some time to come. In fact, the prefrontal cortex of his brain, which is located just behind his forehead, will not fully mature until he is eighteen to twenty-one years old.

How the Brain Grows

The human brain begins life as a small cluster of cells in the fetus. Around the fourth month of pregnancy, these cells begin to sort themselves out according to the function they will one day perform; they then begin to migrate to the part of the brain they are designed to occupy. Some of the cells do not survive the migration; others join together in networks of connections called synapses.

Your son's brain continues to grow at an astonishing pace after he is born. By the time he is two, his brain will have the same number of synapses as yours. By the time he is three, he will have more than one thousand trillion connections—twice as many as his parents. As you may recall from Chapter 3, it is relationship and experience that shape the wiring of the brain, so your son will depend on you for the connection and care that helps him develop.

 **Fact**

> Researchers recently confirmed the existence in humans of mirror neurons, cells within the human brain that are designed to record and imitate both physical movement and emotion. When you play "peek-a-boo" with your baby boy or wave "bye-bye," his mirror neurons record your movements and prime his brain to duplicate them, beginning the lifelong process of communication, learning, and empathy.

Researchers believe that early experience—such as hugs from a favorite grandparent, splashing in a cold pool, or playing with finger foods—actually stimulates the growth of synapses. The brain is amazingly resilient and flexible and can adjust surprisingly well to change or injury early in life. Still, there appear to be windows during a child's growth when important skills such as language are acquired. Brain development is a "use it or lose it" proposition for some functions, and what is used depends largely on you.

Encourage Your Son's Brain Development

Parents across cultures and through the ages have instinctively understood how to nurture and support the healthy growth of their babies. As it turns out, much of what parents do naturally with babies seems especially designed to stimulate healthy brain growth. The Reiner Foundation and Parents' Action for Children offer the following suggestions for ways to connect with your baby that will also support healthy brain development:

- **Respond to your baby's cues.** As you have learned, responding appropriately to the signals your baby sends is called contingent communication and is vital to his development. It is never wise to ignore a crying baby. Check him first, and then decide what to do.
- **Touch, speak, and sing.** Holding, cuddling, talking, and singing songs communicate love and prepare your baby to learn language and social skills.
- **Provide opportunities to play.** Play is your child's work and how he will learn about his body, movement, and the world around him. You don't need fancy baby toys; a game of "patty cake" or crawling together on the floor will do just fine.
- **Encourage curiosity and safe exploration.** Your son will need room to move in order to learn about his body (and gravity). Childproof your home, and then let him explore while you watch and encourage.
- **Allow private time for your baby.** Too much stimulation can make even the calmest baby cranky. Be sure your son has time to sit and watch, to explore his own body, and to calm himself down. With experience, you will find the right balance between interaction and allowing him time to himself.

- **Use discipline to teach—never shake or hit.** Fear and pain do not promote love and healthy learning, especially in the early years. You will learn more about discipline in the pages ahead; for now, be sure never to use physical force to "discipline" your baby.

- **Take care of yourself.** Your son can read your emotions and state of mind better than you guess. Stress, exhaustion, or depression will affect your relationship. Maternal depression can affect a baby's brain development, especially after the first six months. Caring for yourself should always be a top priority in parenting your son.

- **Select child care carefully.** As you will learn, quality child care can actually benefit children, but it is vitally important that you choose your son's caregivers wisely. Parents and caregivers should work together to promote healthy development in young children.

- **Love and enjoy your child.** Remember, your son needs to know that he belongs and has worth and significance. No matter how busy you may be, never forget to tickle, laugh, and hug. Love is the most important connection of all.

(For more information on parenting and brain growth in the early years, see Parents' Action for Children at *www.parentsaction.org*.)

Your Son's Emotional Development

It may come as a surprise to many parents, but boys have just as many emotions (and feel them just as intensely) as girls do. In fact, as you have learned, boys may actually be more emotionally vulnerable and sensitive early in life than girls are. Emotion (rather than logic and reason) is the energy that drives the human brain. Your son's first year is an excellent time to begin building what Dan Kindlon, Ph.D., and Michael Thompson, Ph.D., call emotional literacy, your boy's ability to understand and express emotions clearly.

One of the earliest pioneers in the study of human development was Erik Erikson. Erikson believed that the first emotional task a child must master is trust: the knowledge that his parents and care-givers will come when he needs them and that the routines of daily life will happen predictably and safely. Children who have been abused or who have been in and out of foster care during their early lives may lack this important ability; some children are unwilling even to make eye contact with adults or tolerate physical close-ness. Not surprisingly, trust is an important component in building a secure attachment.

Question?

What if my son cries whenever I put him down?
Babies need attention, however, if you begin feeling like a slave to your son, you may want to look for a better balance between hold-ing him and leaving him to soothe and entertain himself. Sometimes a friendly touch or a loving word will be enough to calm him down.

You may have taken great care to decorate your son's room and to provide stimulating toys and things to look at. Your son's favorite object, however, is your face; infants prefer looking at human faces to any other thing. Gazing at your son and allowing him face time with you prepares him to interpret both your emotions and his own. Smile at him and watch him smile back; coo and sing and he is likely to respond with pleasure.

Many studies have found that parents spend more time talking to baby girls than they do boys; most parents tend to choose physical play with their infant sons, bouncing them, tickling them, or moving their arms and legs. Other studies have shown that boys who receive less affection tend to have greater problems with behavior in pre-school. Be sure you take lots of time to talk and cuddle face to face with your boy.

Your Son's Cognitive Development

You may have encountered parents whose goal is to make their child a genius from day one by surrounding him with academic stimulation. Imagine a couple named Miriam and Peter, who are thrilled when their son Jacob is born—and determined to give him the best possible start in life. They buy stacks of books about infant development; they read to Jacob constantly and play classical music and jazz for him while he plays and naps. Jacob's room is decorated with an ABC motif, and when he begins to crawl, Miriam labels the furniture and other items in the house with the appropriate words. As Jacob crawls around his world, he finds words like "chair," "bunny," and "table" right at eye level. Peter and Miriam are convinced that Jacob will be reading by the age of three. If they have anything to do with it, Jacob will be an academic superstar.

 **Fact**

> Susan Gilbert reports in *A Field Guide to Boys and Girls* that the number of words spoken to an infant each day is the single most important predictor of the child's intelligence, academic success, and social abilities in the years ahead. Talking appears to stimulate the formation of connections in a child's growing brain.

All parents want their children to succeed in life. But do babies really need flashcards and formal teaching?

Actually, no. Babies do not need formal education. Most early learning happens in the context of relationship; your baby boy needs connection with you. As it happens, reading together and exploring the world around you are wonderful ways to encourage an aptitude for language and learning.

Believe it or not, television (even "educational" television) does not encourage the development of language skills. Your son will learn language through conversation with you, by listening to your speech and by beginning to imitate you. You can sit with your son in your lap and look at board books together: Point to the objects in the book and name them. Everyday life can become a wonderful laboratory for learning as you share words and ideas together. But there is no need to force or push this early learning; in fact, some experts believe that forcing children to learn before they're ready may actually make it more difficult for them to learn later on.

Alert!

One recent study found that mothers encouraged language skills equally in male and female infants until around the age of eight months. However, mothers of boy babies, who often become more physically active around that age, began to emphasize language less and to let their sons focus more on physical development than on verbal skills.

Perhaps the best way to encourage learning in your small son is to love learning yourself and to share with your boy the things that fascinate you. You can listen to music together, enjoy books and pictures, and chat about the world around you. You can play and talk while you're playing. No, he won't follow every word, but he will learn from the sound of your voice and the expressions on your face. The best teaching in this first year is your loving and connected relationship with your son.

Temperament

Each child born is a unique and special person. Not surprisingly, each parent is unique, too. One of the most important tasks you face in raising your boy is learning to understand his special qualities, his strengths, and yes, his weaknesses. He has both, and so do you. As you live and grow together, you will become more aware of the traits that make your son who he is.

Most experts now believe that temperament traits are inborn; they appear not to change much over the course of a person's life span. In other words, there are some aspects of your son's nature and personality that are simply part of the package; you cannot change them and will have to learn to work with them. Some parents and children appear to fit together as easily as peas in a pod; others will struggle for years to find connection and understanding. Why are some babies "easy" while others pose a daily challenge to their confused parents?

 Essential

Drs. Chess and Thomas explored the concept of goodness of fit, the idea that a child's temperament, his environment, and his parents' approach to parenting do not always mesh smoothly. Parents can learn to adapt their parenting styles to their child's unique temperament (rather than blaming the child or themselves), improving the fit and helping everyone get along better.

Stella Chess, M.D., and Alexander Thomas, M.D., pioneered the idea that inborn traits may influence a child's behavior. Drs. Chess and Thomas, a husband and wife team, became fascinated by the differences in human personality and behavior and began a study that lasted for decades. Babies, they believe, come into the world already equipped with a set of characteristics and traits that shape their reaction to the world around them. What appears to be difficult behavior can often be explained as the way a child's temperament expresses itself in his family and surroundings.

There are nine different dimensions of temperament, according to Drs. Chess and Thomas. Each is a continuum, and with time and familiarity, you will be able to identify your son on each dimension. Put together, these nine dimensions of temperament will help you understand your son and parent him wisely and lovingly.

1. **Activity.** Some children are quiet by nature, while others never stop moving. And not all active children are "hyperactive." Knowing your son's activity level will help you plan his day and allow for his need for movement (or quiet).
2. **Intensity.** Your son may be reserved by nature, or he may express himself in dramatic extremes. If your son is intense by nature, your job will be to help him calm down and use words to express his needs and feelings. If he is less intense, you may need to focus on drawing him out.
3. **Sensitivity.** Your son may never notice that he is walking barefoot across hot gravel. Or he may flinch at the elastic in his clothing and insist that his socks are too tight. Sensitivity measures your boy's ability to handle visual, auditory, and physical stimulation. He may love a crowd or crave quiet time, and he may need your help occasionally in getting what he needs.
4. **Regularity.** Eighteen-month-old Timmy eats all his meals on schedule and has a bowel movement at the same time every morning; his cousin Peter never follows the same routine twice. Timmy is regular, and life is much simpler for his parents than for Peter's. Regularity refers to a child's bodily functions and need for sleep, food, and bathroom time.
5. **Persistence.** This dimension measures a child's willingness to stay focused on a task despite frustration or lack of immediate success. Understanding your son's tolerance for frustration will give you insight about how best to teach and support him.
6. **Distractibility.** Your son may be able to tune out the television, radio, and your conversation with friends to focus on

his game or book. Or he may be distracted by every noise and movement in the room. Distractibility is often a factor in how well a child performs in school.

7. **Approach or withdrawal.** Some babies accept new people, foods, and toys eagerly, while others turn their heads away or refuse to try something new. If your son is slow to approach, you can help him best by showing patience and acceptance and by teaching coping skills as he grows.

8. **Adaptability.** You may be blessed with a baby who will go anywhere, sleep anywhere, nurse anywhere, and be happy anywhere. Or you may have an infant who desperately needs familiar surroundings and people to feel secure. Children low in adaptability will need extra help from parents as they experience change in their daily routines.

9. **Mood.** Some children (like some adults) see the glass as half empty, while others see it as half full. Mood—the tendency toward optimism or negativity—appears to be an inborn trait. Rather than blaming or trying to fix your little one, you can work on ways to help him see the positive side of life.

Remember, temperament traits are no one's fault—including your son's. They appear to be part of the package human beings are born with, and wise parents will learn to shape, encourage, and teach rather than blame, lecture, or nag. Knowing your son's comfort level and preferences will give you clues about how to make each day as enjoyable and easy as possible. Knowing your own temperament will help you plan for the times when you don't fit and accept them as part of the process of raising your son.

The Importance of Touch for Boys

Boys need hugs. And for many parents, particularly fathers, offering loving touch to boys may feel wrong. If you hold your son too often, will it make him soft? Will you spoil him? If you offer him hugs and cuddles, will he be less masculine as he grows up?

Babies who are massaged, touched, and held often are less irritable and gain weight more quickly than babies who are not touched. Touch is a powerful means of communication, especially with an infant who does not yet understand words.

The Power of Touch

Touch is one of the first messages your son receives from you: If you are happy to see him and pleased with his behavior, you are likely to touch him gently, lovingly, and perhaps for longer. If he has cried all afternoon and refused to take a nap, and now you have to change his diaper, your touch may be rougher, brisker, and less affectionate. Either way, your little boy is learning about you, about himself, and about what works in his new family.

Challenges of Touch for Fathers

Touch can be difficult for many fathers, who may not have experienced loving touch from their own parents or who may believe the subtle messages of our culture that boys should somehow need less physical affection and contact than girls. Yet study after study has shown that fathers are crucial to their sons' emotional and intellectual development. If you are the father of a baby boy, you can help him best by being directly involved in his care. Take time to change diapers and to comfort him when he cries. Smile at him, hold him, and rock him. Wrestling and roughhousing are great, but be sure there is time for tender touch as well.

As your son grows, touch may be more effective than words in communicating love and encouragement. Ruffling your son's hair, rubbing his back, and offering him a hug when life is overwhelming are all ways of building connection and sending the message of love.

Do Babies Need Discipline?

Active, healthy babies do many things that worry, annoy, or irritate their parents. Your son is busy learning all about the world around him, and everything is an exciting experiment. Dropping toys and food is a great way to learn about gravity; ripping paper makes noise and feels good. Your son does not yet feel completely comfortable in his own body, so each day may be a little different from the one before it. He may decide that shrieking is entertaining and do it for hours. He may love to climb the furniture. And for some reason, little boys are quick to discover remote controls and telephones. Sometimes parents worry that without discipline, their small son will become a brat.

You may be pleased to know that you can relax about discipline, especially during the first year of your son's life. He does not need discipline in the traditional sense; in fact, when most parents talk about discipline, they really *mean* punishment. And babies do not need punishment at all.

The literal meaning of the word "discipline" is "to teach." In fact, the word comes from the same Latin root as the word "disciple." What your son needs during his first year—and in fact, throughout your years together—is lots and lots of teaching. And teaching happens best where there is patience, kindness, and respect.

 **Fact**

Babies do not yet have the ability to connect cause and effect, so tools such as time-out and consequences will not work. The best discipline for your baby boy is lots of supervision, physically removing him from things he should not touch, and redirecting him toward acceptable activities.

Parents often believe that a boy requires more discipline than a girl, and sometimes are quick to use physical means to "teach him a lesson." However, your son will learn to respect limits (and you) as he acquires language and emotional skills, and as he builds a loving and respectful relationship with you. Most of the time, a firm voice and the willingness to get up and gently move your baby away from forbidden objects are the best approach—and yes, you will have to do it more than once. Words alone are never effective discipline with a young child, and yelling will only make both of you feel terrible. Kind, firm action and lots of teaching are best.

Child Care

Like it or not, most families these days have two working parents. Even if you are able to have a parent at home with your son, there will inevitably be times when you need to find child care for him, perhaps so that you and your partner can spend some time together. Single parents, too, need to find reliable care, as staying home with a baby is usually not an option. How can you be sure that the person or facility that you leave your beloved son with is going to take good care of him?

There are many ways to provide care for your son when you cannot be with him. You may find a babysitter or family member to come into your home. You may find someone who provides care in her own home. Or you may choose a child care center with special facilities and a trained staff.

Not surprisingly, the same qualities that are important to effective parenting are important in quality child care. Whoever you choose to care for your son, that person or facility should be adequately trained, should have a solid knowledge of child development, and should have a philosophy of discipline that you feel comfortable with.

Here are some things to consider when choosing care for your son:

- If you choose a sitter to come to your home, is that person trained in CPR and infant care?
- Have you provided contact information and special instructions about caring for your baby?
- Can a sitter provide references for your review?
- If you choose an in-home provider, is that person licensed?
- If you plan to take your son to a child care facility, is it clean and well-appointed?

- Is the child care center licensed and/or accredited?
- Ask to observe before leaving your son at a center: Does the staff know how to communicate with young children?
- Has the staff at the center been trained in early childhood education and development?

You should also find out how a child care center deals with discipline, and whether it is a pleasant and child-friendly place. (For more information about selecting child care, see the Web site of the National Association for the Education of Young Children at *www.naeyc.org.*)

The quality of the child care you provide for your baby is vitally important; in many cases, child care providers spend as much (if not more) time with children than their parents do. Inadequate care may jeopardize the health, safety, and development of your son, but quality care may actually enhance his learning and development of social skills. Whether you leave your baby for work or to have some time to yourself, he has the opportunity to learn that when you leave him, you always return and are happy to see him again. Child care is a necessity in the lives of most families; just be sure that the care you provide during your son's early years is the best that you can find.

CHAPTER 5

Your Preschool Boy

Y ou may be dreading the "terrible twos." Perhaps you're worried about the "tyrannical threes." If you've spent any time at all around preschool boys, you probably won't be surprised to learn that human beings never have more physical energy than they do at the age of three. There is no question that little boys can be a handful; they are energetic, impulsive, and funny. They are curious and occasionally defiant. But they are also charming and compassionate. Welcome to the world of the preschool boy!

Creating a Safe Environment

While it's never wise to generalize about human beings, there are definitely a few things parents can learn from the differences between boys and girls during the preschool years, roughly the ages of eighteen months to six years old. Most of the available research tells us that as a group, little boys tend to be more physically active, competitive, and yes, aggressive than little girls. If you always expect your toddler son to sit quietly in a restaurant or in church and follow the rules, you will be disappointed at least some of the time.

Boys like to *move*. Before their first birthdays, they experience a surge of physical energy that will last for quite some time. Each boy is an individual, and one of the most important tasks you face as a parent is learning to know and understand *your* unique son. Still, most boys do love to run, climb, wrestle, dig, and explore. If

there's a locked drawer or a dark closet, sooner or later your son is likely to discover it, and he will want to unearth its secrets.

A Voyage of Self-Discovery

You will need to remind yourself often during these busy years that your little boy truly does not plan to defy or frustrate you. Young children do not acquire the ability to tie cause and effect together, to make formal plans, or to think things through reasonably until they are around three years old. It may appear that your son deliberately sets out each day to do all the things you have specifically forbidden, but that really is not what is happening.

Alert!

Boys' inability to control their impulses not only creates daredevil and defiant behavior when they're young, it can lead to problems with drug and alcohol abuse, promiscuity, and defiance of authority later on. These early years are the time to build a respectful relationship with your son and to practice setting reasonable limits.

Life in your son's world is an ongoing experiment, a marvelous laboratory where he can learn about himself, others, and the world he inhabits. And little boys learn by *doing*, by touching and holding and throwing. Your son is busy learning about himself; your job as his parent is to supervise, protect, set reasonable limits when necessary, and follow through with kindness, firmness, and respect.

The Argument for Childproofing

Some parents believe that a house should never be childproofed. Instead, they claim, the child should be "house-proofed," taught never to touch fragile items or enter off-limits rooms. Many of these same parents then spend much of their free time in power struggles with their little boys, lecturing, enforcing, slapping hands, and mourning the loss of Grandma's crystal.

Boys certainly need to learn to respect limits and to look without touching. But learning these skills is a process that takes time and patience. In the meantime, wise parents learn to create some safe space for their active little boys. Here are some suggestions:

Safety Comes First

Be sure that as soon as your son becomes mobile you cover electrical outlets, put latches on drawers and cupboards, and put chemicals and cleaning supplies well out of reach. Check electrical appliances to be sure they can't be turned on and that cords are not frayed or easily chewed on. It is also wise to use safety gates around stairways and to be sure that pools are fenced. Accidents are a constant danger to curious little ones; be sure you take the time to prevent as many as you can.

Put Breakables Out of Reach

Keep breakable items away from your son, at least for now. Your three-year-old may "know" that he shouldn't touch your china figurines, but he just *can't* resist holding one. Your son's sense of belonging and safety is more valuable than even the most precious collection. Put the fragile items away until he has better impulse control. It will save you many painful (and unnecessary) arguments.

Create Safe Spaces

Make sure you have created childproof areas of your home where your son is welcome to play and explore. You may want to leave the pantry or a cupboard unlatched so your son can stack cans or play with the plastic containers. If you can handle the noise, pots and pans make great drum sets, and most little boys love to bang away from time to time. Or you can set up a play space in a corner of a family area where you can be sure your son is protected and where there are items he will enjoy. Remember, things to manipulate, stack, connect, or hammer are usually good choices.

Make Time for Active Play

It can be helpful to build time into every day for your son to run, climb, and be physically active in acceptable, safe ways. Quiet times will work better for both of you when he's also had time to zoom.

Perhaps your little boy should be able to behave nicely. In time, kind and firm parenting and discipline designed to teach will encourage him to do so. In the meantime, while your son learns about his world, do your best to keep him (and your valuables) safe by creating a home that is inviting and safe for both of you.

Language and Social Skills

It may come as something of a surprise to you, but children have to learn how to play. Your son's earliest playmates will undoubtedly be you and the children he encounters at preschool, at your friends' homes, and at the park. In these early encounters, play is more likely to be conducted side by side than face to face.

Social skills are among the many things children must learn, and if you've ever tried to encourage three- or four-year-olds to share, you know how challenging the process can be. Children must learn how to get along with others and to gain a sense of what others are feeling and thinking—what Daniel Siegel, M.D., calls mindsight. The process takes time and a great deal of patience and coaching from parents.

Very young children engage in what is called parallel play. That is, they tend to sit together, each playing independently. They are in the same space, and they are playing—but they are not playing together. Eventually, a child will begin to notice other children and to express curiosity about these strange beings. A little boy is likely to explore his new acquaintance by touching or poking him or by grabbing at a toy to see what he will do.

Language and Play

Not surprisingly, social relationships tend to work out better when a child has learned to use his words. It also helps when a child has acquired some emotional skills and can read faces and body language to understand whether or not to approach a new person. It has been noted in several studies that girls tend to be more collaborative in their play; they talk and make rules together about how their game will go. Boys often form groups with a leader, and the chosen activity is usually physical.

 Essential

One psychologist found that mothers of daughters talk more with their children about sadness and ways to solve problems; mothers of sons talk about anger and ways to get even. Use curiosity questions with your son to help him understand feelings and resolve conflicts with his friends.

Your son will need time and opportunity to practice his social skills. Be sure you offer him opportunities to be with children his own age. When things go awry (and they inevitably will), don't punish or scold; instead, take time to explore with your son what happened, what made it happen, and what he could do to get a better result next time. Parents can help with the development of social skills by coaching children with their friends, rather than intervening.

Hitting and Aggression

Boys are certainly more prone to physical aggression, even bullying, than are girls. They may kick, bite, or throw things when they feel frustrated or defeated. Speech experts believe that some aggressive activity may be related to the development of language; children who are slower to speak clearly often experience frustration and express it in the form of anger or defiance.

Your son needs to learn that hurting himself, another person, or property is never acceptable. But hurting *him* will not teach that lesson. Instead, always take a moment to calm down first, and then help him do the same. (You will learn more about positive time-out later on.) Remove your son gently from the situation or other children if necessary. Then, when both you and he are able to talk, look together for solutions to the problem.

If other children are involved, it is helpful to explore what they might have been feeling. You can also tell your son how you are feeling, "I feel sad and worried when you kick the dog." Or, "It hurts when you hit me, and I cannot allow you to do that." Stay calm; raising your own voice never helps.

The Art of Sharing

Sharing is difficult. In fact, you may know several adults who can't do it very well. For young children (who haven't yet accepted that they are not the center of the family universe), it's often downright impossible. Sharing becomes important to parents and teachers as children reach the age of three or four and are more likely to have younger siblings or to be part of groups of children. "Share with your little sister," you might say to your son. Unfortunately, until he's had some training and practice, he is likely to respond by jutting out his lip and pulling harder on his toy.

You can help your son learn to share by taking time to teach. Remember, your son does not know how to negotiate or compromise and may not have a fully functional vocabulary (or a great deal of self-control). You can model sharing by showing him what it looks like: "Here's a cookie. I'll have a piece, and I'll share a piece with you." Or you can show him how to take turns: "I'll throw the ball to you, and then you throw it to me."

You can also coach children to use words together. For example, you might say, "I can see that you want Jessie's toy. What could you say to her?" If your son says, "Please, may I have the toy?" you can smile, and then help Jessie figure out how to respond. (Please note that the answer does not always have to be yes. "Maybe later" is an appropriate answer, too.)

Like most of the skills and concepts adults take for granted, sharing is an art that must be practiced over and over again. As in so many other areas of life with your son, you can be his best teacher and example.

 **Fact**

Brain researchers tell us that autobiographical memory, called explicit memory, does not develop until a child is approximately two years old. Until then, your son's sense of self and sense of time is not like yours; he is probably telling you the truth when he tells you that he "can't remember" something that happened.

It will take lots of practice for your son to learn to get along easily with his peers, and even the best of friends sometimes disagree. Keep your cool, keep everyone safe, and be prepared to do lots of patient teaching as your son learns about friendship.

Getting into Your Son's World

Even the most loving parent sometimes assumes that a young child thinks, feels, and experiences life as adults do. Nothing could be farther from the truth. Sometime soon, try the following experiment: Get down on your knees. (Yes, really.) Now "walk" from your son's bedroom to the kitchen. How long does it take you to get there? What do you see along the way? Is it easy to reach the things you need? If there is an adult handy, look up at her. Wow, she's pretty big, isn't she? What does she look like if she's angry?

Now imagine going for a walk to the park. Imagine holding the adult's hand and notice how soon you want to pull your own hand away—not because you're feeling defiant but because the blood stops flowing when you hold your arm up too long. Adults walk quickly, don't they? It's hard to keep up, especially when you want to stop and look at the flowers, the cool insect you find in the dirt, or the neighbor's new puppy.

Spending a few moments in your little boy's shoes, or even imagining doing so, can be an immensely helpful experience. Despite what you may have believed, the world of a young child is very different from the world of an adult. Finding ways to understand your son's world may be one of the most valuable parenting tools you will ever learn.

The Value of Curiosity

It isn't easy being a parent. You undoubtedly feel fatigued and stressed at least some of the time; raising your son is almost certainly not the only thing on your daily agenda. Sometimes all you really want is for your son to just listen and to obey without a whimper. Unfortunately, during the preschool years, even the best little boy will struggle to comply with adult expectations. There's just too much else going on in his world.

You will be far more successful at setting limits, communicating, and getting along with your small son when you take time to be curious about who he is becoming and what his world is like. Here are some things to ponder:

- **Preschoolers do not experience time in the same way adults do.** Five minutes for you may feel like an hour for your son. If you expect patience, you will both be disappointed in the results.
- **Preschoolers are far more interested in the process than the product.** You may want a painting to hang on your refrigerator; your son may have found smearing the paint with his fingers satisfying enough, and he may never get around to the final product.
- **Preschoolers cannot tell fantasy from reality the way you can.** If it happens on the movie screen or on television, it's "real" and no amount of debate can convince him otherwise. (This fact is a good reason to exercise caution when the media is concerned.)
- **Preschoolers love to ask questions.** While the constant stream of "whys" and "how comes" can be exhausting, questions are

truly how little boys learn. Be sure to take time to listen to your son, too.

Erik Erikson said there are two stages in children's emotional development during preschool years. At two, they learn autonomy—which is why two-year-olds love saying the word "no." At three, they begin to practice initiative, the ability to make and carry out their own plans. Both of these stages create challenges for parents. Remember that it's normal development and not about you!

Curiosity about your son's perceptions, his feelings, and his ideas is always a good place to begin as you solve problems and face challenges together. It will carry you from the early years through adolescence to the day your son leaves to begin his own independent life. Take time to express curiosity before passing judgment: It will always help you parent your son wisely.

Developmental Appropriateness

Imagine a three-year-old boy named Teddy. He bounces out of bed every morning at six and dashes to the kitchen; he is proud of his ability to make his own breakfast (which means pouring cereal and milk into a bowl and onto the counter and leaving the mess for Mom to clean up). Teddy can operate the remote control, so he watches his favorite cartoons until Mom and Dad appear, bleary-eyed and not nearly as energetic as Teddy is.

Teddy can dress himself, although his shoes aren't always on the right feet and his shorts are usually backward. Teddy is good at taking off his night-time diaper (he isn't toilet-trained yet), but he sometimes forgets to put on a new one. Mom has taught him to comb his hair, but he hates it, so he usually skips that part of his morning. He forgets about brushing his teeth, too, and that usually begins an argument that ends with Teddy screaming, kicking, and crying while Mom waves a loaded toothbrush in front of his clenched lips.

Teddy's tantrums don't last long, though, and soon he is off to play outdoors. He carries his favorite toys into the backyard and leaves them out in the rain when he comes in for lunch. When Mom begins her usual "how many times do I have to tell you" lecture, Teddy concentrates on his juice and yogurt. Teddy plays furiously until Mom says the dreaded word "naptime"; the tantrum that follows exhausts Teddy, and he almost always falls asleep for a little while. "Thank goodness," his mom murmurs quietly, as she carries her grimy, tear-stained boy to his bed.

Teddy is a model of developmental appropriateness, which doesn't always mean his behavior pleases his parents. Teddy's tantrums, his high-energy activity level, his "forgetting" and defiance are normal for boys his age. His mother knows this, and on days when Teddy tries her patience, it helps her to know that he is just doing his job as a small boy.

 **Question?**

What if my son lies?
Your son may lie for many reasons. He may be using his active imagination, or he may know that you will be angry about what happened. You can emphasize responsibility and honesty and still offer him empathy and respect. Focus on finding a solution to the problem rather than blaming him.

Learning about child development will help you take your son's behavior less personally and see it as simply a stage on his journey toward maturity. Parenting classes, child-development classes, or good parenting books, Web sites, and magazines can all be sources of information about why your son does what he does. Understanding developmental appropriateness will allow you to help your son learn the skills and values he needs.

The Terrible Trio

Like it or not, there are three things you simply cannot make a child do. You cannot make him eat, you cannot make him sleep, and you cannot make him use the toilet. Ironically, many of the power struggles parents face with their toddler and preschool boys are about precisely these issues. Anytime a challenge involves your son's body, he is in control of what happens. Your job is to set the stage, teach the skills, and let your son do the rest.

Mealtimes, Snacks, and Other Challenges

Young children and their parents often disagree about eating. Parents tend to like the idea of three meals a day; they want their children to eat healthy food, to eat what is put in front of them without complaining, and to cooperate about snacks and other food choices. Eating is actually much simpler than most parents make it: You should eat when you are hungry and stop when you are full. When parents force children to eat, punish them for avoiding certain foods, provide sugary snacks, or cook meals on demand, they usually interfere with the natural process of eating.

You may worry about your son's eating because you want him to be healthy. It may help you relax to know that children usually eat what they need *over time* (barring illness or other special circumstances). In other words, your son may not eat all of the food groups every day. In fact, he may want to live on macaroni and cheese for days at a time. But if your son is active and healthy, he will usually choose to eat what he needs—eventually.

Supply Healthy Food

Your job is to make good food available; your son's job is to eat it. A little junk food won't damage your son permanently (you don't need to take away his Halloween candy, for instance), but do limit the amount of fatty, sugary treats available. Instead, provide fruits, vegetables, dairy, and other acceptable snacks.

Make Family Meals a Tradition

Try to get your family together for supper each night, but don't force your son to eat. Studies have shown that when a family sits down to eat a meal together at least three times a week, children do better at school, choose better behavior, and are less likely to become involved in drugs or alcohol. Be sure, however, that family meals are a pleasure rather than a battle. It is helpful to provide at least one item that you know your son will eat happily. Invite him to try new things, but don't leave him sitting at the table alone, staring at his unwanted lima beans. He will learn only to resist both you and eating. Focus on connection and conversation.

Get Children Involved

Get your son involved in meal planning, shopping, and food preparation. Children love to be invited; they usually resist being commanded. When your son is old enough, invite him to help you plan meals. You can give him his own short grocery list (use pictures if he cannot read yet) and help him shop. Even toddlers can rinse lettuce, put cheese slices on hamburger buns, and set the table. Your son is more likely to eat something he has helped prepare.

Cooking to Order

Do not cook meals to order! One frazzled mother of three young boys found herself cooking three meals every night. "They won't eat if I don't give them what they want," she said. Providing special service for your son will only create a demand for more of the same. Prepare one meal for the family; if your son refuses to eat it, let him know when the next meal will be. If your son is old enough, you might give him the choice of making himself a sandwich or other simple food. Remember to be kind and firm at the same time.

All children go through phases with their eating, and some actually do better when they are allowed to graze rather than having to wait for the next scheduled meal. Relax and do your best to create peaceful, nourishing mealtimes—and give your son a good multivitamin.

Creating a Healthy Lifestyle

If you have been watching the news recently, you are undoubtedly aware that doctors are increasingly concerned about childhood obesity. Weight gain that happens early in life tends to set patterns that are difficult to change later and may lead to lifelong health problems such as diabetes and hypertension. The preschool years are the perfect time to help your son learn to live a healthy life.

Alert!

It is generally unwise to put your young son on a diet. Pediatricians agree that limiting food intake for growing children tends to set up power struggles and create emotional issues that are often as damaging as the physical ones. It is wiser to focus on the long-term: Pay attention to nutrition, encourage exercise, and get regular check-ups.

Of course, you will always be your son's best teacher. If you sit in front of the television all day snacking on chips and cookies, you will have a hard time convincing him that he shouldn't do the same. If you get regular exercise, eat reasonably healthy food, and limit television, video games, and other passive activities, your son will be more likely to do the same.

The best way to help your boy have an appetite for healthy food is to encourage healthy activity. This can be difficult for working parents whose children are in child care programs, but do your best to keep your son active. Plan fun family activities and enjoy working up a good appetite together.

Nighty-Night—or Not

Sleep, whether at night or during naptime, is another thing you cannot make a child do, but that doesn't stop parents from trying. Who hasn't had one of those evenings when the only thing you want in life is for your beloved son to fall asleep?

Young children learn best by repetition and consistency. Create a routine for any part of your day that is challenging, such as mealtimes, bedtime, or getting out the door in the morning. Make a routine picture chart *with* your son, not for rewards, but to map the order of the activity. Knowing what comes next will help your son cooperate.

You will help your son develop healthy sleep patterns when you learn what helps him relax, and all children are different. Some like a night-light; others want it dark. Some want background noise so they don't feel alone; others need complete silence. Some want to be warm, while others prefer to be cool. There is no right way to sleep; what matters is that your son is comfortable, secure, and relaxed.

Instead of trying to make your son go to sleep, focus on helping him feel sleepy. A game or a walk outdoors before bed may help him feel tired; a warm bath may help him relax. Include stories, songs, and hugs in your bedtime routine. Then, when your son is in bed, give him a kiss and leave him to fall asleep. If he gets up, kindly and firmly return him to his bed. Your son will know when you are serious and when you cannot be manipulated by whining or crying.

 **Question?**

What if my son will fall asleep only in my bed?
Having a snuggle in bed together when your son is sick or has a nightmare is fine, but eventually he will need to learn to sleep on his own. Let him know you want him to sleep in his own room; do his bedtime routine there. It may take time, but be kind and firm.

Your son needs his sleep, but when you're an active little boy, it is hard to slow down long enough to rest. Kindness, firmness, and effective routines will help you create healthy sleep habits.

The Perils of Potty-Training

Here's the news: Boys are generally slower to use the toilet than girls are. In fact, the average age for day and nighttime dryness is around three-and-a-half years old. That may not be good news to moms and dads who are anxious for the diaper days to end. Still, toilet training depends on both physical awareness and self-control, and your son will need to master these abilities before he is successful in the bathroom.

Children have an uncanny ability to sense the issues that are important to parents. If you worry about eating, they will resist food. If you insist on bedtime, they aren't sleepy. And if you make toilet training a battle, they will fight you. Unfortunately, toileting battles can have serious health implications. Forcing your son to use the toilet before he's ready may cause him to withhold his stool, and that can cause severe constipation and an impacted bowel.

To successfully master the bathroom, your son needs to be able to read the physical signals that tell him he has to "go." He needs to be able to undo his buttons or snaps and be willing to leave his play. You can help by letting him see what happens in the bathroom without expecting him to join in. You can provide a diet rich in fiber. And you can understand that your son, too, experiences stress (like the birth of a younger sibling) and that stress may affect his bowel and urination habits.

As with so many other challenges, you must set the stage and encourage your son to do his part. When accidents happen, do your best to remain calm. If appropriate, teach your son to clean himself up without lectures or blame. If you have serious concerns, take time to check with your son's pediatrician. The preschool years are busy, often challenging ones, but they are precious, too. Be sure you take time to enjoy your young son and to preserve memories for the future. Have faith, and as much as you can, have fun.

CHAPTER 6

Discipline as Teaching

Some of the most important questions parents ask about raising a son involve discipline. You probably want to know how to encourage positive, cooperative behavior from your son; you may want to know how to keep him out of trouble as he grows and faces new risks and opportunities. You will certainly want to know how to respond when he is defiant, disrespectful, or careless. But what is effective discipline, anyway?

Discipline and Long-Range Parenting

Remember the list of character qualities you want your son to learn? At its heart, effective and loving discipline will teach your son everything he needs to know about living a successful life, building those qualities into his character step by step and day by day. Discipline involves far more than what to do when your son misbehaves (and he will). Discipline is about teaching your son to live, make good decisions, and solve problems effectively. Consistent discipline teaches trust and shows real love. Discipline, offered with both kindness and firmness, is what will make a good man out of your little boy.

Love and Limits

Everyone must learn to live with limits. Limits create safety and encourage respect in communities and nations; we have laws that forbid theft, murder, and damaging the property of others. Most adults have had

at least one experience with a traffic police officer. You may know the speed limit and may even know that breaking it will cost you a fine (and increased insurance premiums). But sometimes, don't you still drive just a little bit over the limit when you're in a hurry? It's wise to recognize that if you sometimes disregard limits, your growing boy will, too. What matters most is how you respond.

As you consider how to provide the discipline your son will need, it may help to think about the long-range purpose of the limits you set:

- **Arbitrary limits with no obvious purpose will only invite resistance from your son.** Limits are useful to children only when they involve safety or are designed to teach life skills such as cooperation, social skills, responsibility, self-discipline, and respect for others.
- **Your attitude is critical when setting limits for your son.** If you are harsh, punitive, or mean, your son is more likely to learn defiance than cooperation. Limits are most effective when they are set and enforced with an attitude of dignity and respect for everyone involved.
- **If your son is younger than four years old, you are responsible for setting limits.** You decide when he goes to bed, what he may and may not touch, and where he can go.
- **After the age of four, as your son learns to reason and weigh options, he can learn long-range life skills when you involve him in setting limits and understanding the results of his own behavior.** The final decision will be yours, but when children have an opportunity to contribute, they are far more likely to cooperate.

Your son relies on you to think carefully about his future and to set limits that will guide him and encourage him to make good choices in a complicated world.

Permissiveness and Pampering

Imagine a woman named Megan, who is shopping at the local supermarket with her five-year-old son, Kyle. As they wait in line at the checkout stand, Kyle spots a small metal race car on a rack and asks Megan to buy it.

"Please, Mom?" he asks, with his most charming smile. "You can keep my next allowance."

Megan sighs. "Kyle, you've borrowed so much allowance that you won't get any until next month. No toys today."

Kyle, however, is not about to give up so easily. He picks up the car and puts it firmly into the shopping cart. "I *want* it," he says, sticking out his chin and crossing his arms.

"I said no, Kyle." Now Megan is getting angry. Kyle's voice is rising, and so is hers, and other shoppers are beginning to watch their little drama. "If you don't behave right away, you won't get any ice cream after dinner tonight."

"I don't care about your old ice cream," Kyle shouts. "I want my car. I want it now! You're mean. You never let me have anything!" And Kyle begins to scream hysterically.

No question about it now: *Everyone* is watching. Kyle's crumpled face is scarlet and tear-streaked, and Megan wants to crawl under the cart.

"Okay," she hisses at her son, grabbing his elbow. "You can have the car. Just be quiet!"

Now, you certainly would never give in to your son this way. But think about your friends and neighbors who might. What did Kyle *really* learn from his mother's actions? Chances are that he will continue to disregard her limits and beg her for treats because he knows she will give in.

Parents pamper children because they love them. Parents are permissive with children, failing to follow through on limits, because they love them. But pampering and permissiveness do not teach children any useful long-term skills. Instead, children learn selfishness, manipulation, and disrespect for the needs of others. You may enjoy giving your son gifts and treats; you may find it hard to follow through when he disregards limits. But is it really in his long-term best interests to be pampered? Should you hold him accountable for his actions?

 **Fact**

> Daniel Siegel, M.D., says that when a child hears the word "yes," a sort of "accelerator" fires in his brain; when he hears "no," his brain applies the "brakes." Reasonable limits help a child develop an emotional "clutch" that allows him to regulate his impulses and behave in appropriate ways.

Discipline Versus Punishment

Stephen Glenn, Ph.D., a popular speaker and author of several books on raising children, loved to tell the story of a woman who came up to speak to him after a talk about the perils of punishment. "I was punished and spanked," she told Dr. Glenn firmly, "and I turned out just fine." Dr. Glenn looked back at her with a kind smile. "I'm sure you did. But madam, what if you were meant to be superior?"

The Results of Punishment

Punishment is something a more powerful person does to a less powerful person in the hope of creating a change in behavior. In fact, our entire criminal justice system relies on punishment, although punishment rarely "cures" the criminal. Parents rely on punishments such as spanking, slapping, verbal insults, taking away privileges and possessions, grounding, and humiliation in the belief that they will teach children to avoid poor choices and bad behavior. And in the short term, punishment does appear to work: After all, when you spank a child, he does stop doing what he's doing for at least a while.

Unfortunately, the long-term results of punishment and excessive control are not encouraging. A great deal of research reveals that punishment tends to create the opposite of what committed, loving parents hope to create. Murray Straus, Ph.D., of the University of New Hampshire Family Research Laboratory, conducted a long-range study that followed families in which spanking was used by conscientious, nonabusive parents to manage children's behavior. Straus discovered that although the families initially reported that the spanking "worked," over time those same families reported more incidences of misbehavior and disrespect in their children. Another study shows that kindergartners who are spanked at home, even mildly, are more likely to be physically aggressive at school or to bully their peers.

Alert!

A recent study of public school administrators found that African-American boys are the group most likely to be physically punished at school, but in all ethnic groups boys are much more likely to be hit than girls. Judges also commit boys to juvenile detention centers more often than girls who commit the same offenses.

There is also research that shows that when punishments that create fear or shame are used, a child is more likely to remember the emotion he experienced than the intended lesson. Over time, punishment and excessive control can create defiance, rebellion, and resistance, or sneakiness and passivity. None of these qualities are likely to be on the list you made for your own son. As Dan Kindlon, Ph.D, and Michael Thompson, Ph.D., point out, when a boy experiences harsh punishment, he loses much of his openness to empathy, conscience, and connection with others.

What about Rewards?

Well, you may be thinking, perhaps punishment isn't such a good idea for my son. But certainly a few rewards won't hurt. Don't children learn faster when they have the opportunity to earn a treat of some kind? Rewards are woven throughout our schools and families: Teachers give out stickers, special privileges, and small toys. Parents make detailed charts and encourage children to do chores, earn good grades, and behave well to earn rewards. Most of these well-meaning adults would be shocked to discover that rewards actually stifle performance and discourage children from trying new things and learning new skills.

 **Fact**

Excessive control leads children to develop an external locus of control. Meaning, their behavior depends on who is watching and whether a punishment or reward is involved. Kind, firm discipline leads children to develop an internal locus of control, the ability to do the right thing "just because."

Rewards teach children to perform in order to receive something. The danger of rewards is that over time, children usually up the ante. In other words, the boy who would mow the lawn for a dollar when he was ten wants five dollars when he's twelve. Alfie Kohn puts it this way in his excellent, research-based book *Punished by Rewards*: "What rewards and punishment do produce is *temporary compliance*. They buy us obedience. If that's what we mean when we say they 'work,' then yes, they work wonders. But if we are ultimately concerned with the kind of people our children will become . . . no behavioral manipulation ever helped a child develop a commitment to becoming a caring and responsible person." If punishment and rewards won't help your son achieve the qualities on your list, then what will?

Kind, Firm Discipline That Teaches

Discipline is a crucial decision for all parents, regardless of the gender of their children. But clearly, parents of boys need to think about what they want to teach, and what their sons will learn. Discipline, at heart, is very simple. Effective discipline will teach your son moral values, the ability to know right from wrong, to work hard, to love and respect others, to have integrity, and to be responsible and capable.

Effective discipline can be as simple as a conversation or it may require a consequence that you have agreed on in advance with your son. Discipline can and should be kind and firm at the same time. And effective, loving discipline will allow your boy to trust you, to stay connected to you, to respect you, and to learn what he must about how to get along in the world. Real discipline gives a boy what he needs, rather than just what he wants.

Following Through

For many parents, setting limits and making rules is the easy part of discipline; the hard part is usually following through. Grandma's old-fashioned advice—say what you mean and mean what you say—is still true. Why do so many parents struggle to remain kind and firm, and to follow through on limits and agreements with respect and dignity?

Well, many parents worry that if they mean it when they set limits, their children somehow will not love them as much. It's much more pleasant to be nice; many parents would rather be a child's friend than a parent. But as we have seen, your son relies on you to teach him the character and skills he will need to have a successful life.

Following through with dignity and respect, kindness and firmness, is one of the most loving things you can do for your son. You will learn more specific ideas as you read the chapters ahead, but there are some things you should always keep in mind about discipline.

Appropriate Limits and Motivation

Be sure limits and expectations are developmentally appropriate. Your son's age, temperament, and development have a strong influence on his behavior. Be sure you know what he is capable of *before* setting limits. Much misbehavior, especially in the early years, has more to do with development than poor choices.

In addition to knowing the appropriate limits to set for your son according to his stage of development, you will also benefit from trying to understand where he is coming from. Try to understand the beliefs behind your son's behavior. Your boy may have decided that he gets more of your attention when he misbehaves. Or he may feel a sense of belonging and significance only when he is showing you that you can't control him. Take a moment to consider what your son believes about his behavior and what you want him to learn.

Belonging and Solutions

A misbehaving child is a discouraged child. When your son misbehaves, he may believe it is the only way to create a connection with you. Find ways to encourage him and to understand what's going on for him. When he feels belonging, his behavior will improve.

You must also focus on solutions rather than consequences (or punishments). It isn't helpful to focus on blame or to create elaborate consequences. If your son is older than four or so, you can talk with him about problems and make agreements about what should happen. Be sure that your actions *solve the problem*, rather than making your son feel badly. Ask your son, "What ideas do you have for solving this problem?" Children can be amazingly creative when given the chance.

Alert!

Yelling is never helpful and never necessary. All parents do it from time to time, but the less yelling you do, the more cooperative your son is likely to be. Boys sometimes enjoy having the power to make a parent "lose it"; be sure you take care of yourself so you can stay calm.

If a consequence is necessary, be sure your son knows about it *in advance* and that you can follow through. For instance, you may agree that if your son leaves toys on the living room floor after clean-up time, you will pick them up and put them in a box for two days. If you have to follow through (and you probably will), don't lecture or nag: Simply put the toys away with kindness and firmness. Later you can talk about what should happen next time.

Training and Meetings

Your son wasn't born knowing how to clean his room. Take time to teach him the skills he needs to do what you expect, and do your best to keep your expectations reasonable. When your son is young, you can work beside him to teach him; later on, he will know how to do the job himself.

In addition to taking the time and energy to train your son, you should set aside periods for regular family meetings. If your son is older than four, set a time each week to gather as a family. Begin with compliments for tasks done well; post an agenda board where family members can list problems they need help with. Work together to find solutions and make agreements. You can check at the next meeting to see how your plan is working. End with a shared dessert, game, or other family fun.

Connection and Learning

Remember the importance of connection. Take time to listen, to play, and just to hang out with your boy. When he feels connected to you and has a sense of belonging and significance, he is less likely to misbehave.

It is also helpful to remember that mistakes are opportunities to learn. Mistakes—yours and your son's—are inevitable. Mistakes are not horrible failures; they are opportunities to learn better ways of solving problems. Clean up the mess, and then talk together about how to solve the problem. Blaming and shaming are not necessary. (For more specific information on discipline at various ages, see the *Positive Discipline* series by Jane Nelsen, Ed.D., and others.)

Encouraging Communication

As you and your son grow together, you will discover that the best discipline is prevention, understanding yourself and your son well enough to anticipate problems. Most parents have said, "He just doesn't listen!" at one time or another, but they are sometimes surprised to learn that children often feel the same way. Choosing words carefully and listening attentively will help you build a strong and caring relationship with your son.

The Power of Active Listening

Think of this situation to help you recognize the benefits of actively listening to your son. Steve was finishing up some work at the computer when he heard the front door open, then slam shut. As the walls of the house reverberated, he heard footsteps pounding down the hall and the slamming of yet another door: Joshua's room.

Steve swallowed a heavy sigh and managed not to yell, "Don't slam the doors!" He'd had a long day at work and was already tired; he didn't feel like dealing with his thirteen-year-old son's temper. Steve took a moment to calm himself, and then walked to his son's door.

"Joshua?" he asked quietly. "What's up?"

"Go away," came the curt reply.

Steve paused. "You know, I heard the door slam when you came in. You must be feeling pretty angry about something."

There was a long silence from the other side of the door. Then it cracked open and Joshua's sullen face peered out. His chin was trembling; he was obviously trying not to cry. Somehow the sight of his son's pain melted the last of Steve's anger.

"Can I come in, Josh?" he asked. When Joshua nodded, Steve took a seat on the bed and looked up into his son's face.

"You look pretty sad," he said simply.

Joshua exploded. "Peter and Allen got hold of a couple of beers," he said. "They dared me to drink with them after school, and when I said no, they called me a mama's boy." He stifled a sob. "They don't even know that my mom is dead, but it still made me so mad. And it made me miss her all over again." Joshua collapsed on the bed next to his dad and put his head in his hands.

Steve felt a wave of relief that he hadn't yelled at Joshua about the door; he wordlessly slipped an arm around his son's shoulders.

"I'm glad you refused the beer. And I know you still miss Mom; so do I. I think we'll miss her for a long time." Steve sat silently holding his son until Joshua straightened and looked up at him. "Let's go get a pizza, shall we?" Steve said, giving his son a last squeeze.

Dealing with Feelings

Feelings are a vital part of communication. And as you will learn in Chapter 7, boys often struggle to identify and express feelings in positive ways. Steve used active listening to create connection with Joshua, rather than conflict.

 **Question?**

What if my son got into a fight at school, and he was disciplined at school? Should I also discipline him at home?

If the principal handled the problem effectively and your son has learned not to fight, adding consequences at home may create resentment. Instead, sit down with your son and ask him what happened and why. Practice active listening and look together for solutions.

Active listening means taking time to notice what your son is *feeling* and identifying that emotion, without attempting to fix or change it. Active listening creates a sense of being understood and can help you avoid arguments and misunderstandings with your son. Even when your son chooses not to talk about what he is feeling, you are sending the message that you care.

It certainly takes self-control not to react with anger when your son provokes you. If you can remain calm, however, and focus on active listening, you may find you need the other tools of discipline far less often.

Emotional Honesty

Parents have lots of feelings, too. You may experience dozens of emotions in a single day, from frustration to worry to joy. What should you do with your own feelings when it's time to discipline your son?

Remember, discipline is teaching. Your son can learn a great deal about respect and managing emotions from how you respond to challenging moments. Covering up or denying your own feelings rarely works; children can read nonverbal signals and usually know quite well how you feel.

It can be helpful to express your own feelings, but to do so in a constructive way. For instance, you might say, "I'm feeling frustrated because we're late for school and the car has a flat tire. I'd appreciate it if you could help me by packing up your books and papers." Or, "When you come home late and don't call me, I feel worried because you might be hurt. I'd appreciate a phone call next time." (If you need to take a deep breath before speaking, feel free.) Listening well and speaking clearly and calmly will help you avoid a great deal of conflict with your son.

Positive Time-Out

"You stop that or you're in time-out!" "One, two, three. . ." "Go to time-out and think about what you did!" What parent hasn't heard of and tried time-out? And what parent hasn't occasionally found herself spending even more time trying to keep a wriggling, defiant boy in time-out? Time-out is one of the most common discipline tools, and one of the most misused. Many parents use time-out with an attitude of punishment, so it shouldn't be surprising that so many children resist it. Truth is, time-out can be helpful for both parent and child, but only when it is understood and used correctly.

Taking the Low Road

Right in the center of your brain is a system informally known as the stress response system. Its job is to generate emotions and to sense and respond to threats. When you believe yourself to be in danger, this system diverts energy to the parts of your body necessary to defend yourself, sometimes called "fight or flight." It is an involuntary system, which means that it is not under your conscious control. Every human being has one of these systems—including your son.

When you lose your temper, your prefrontal cortex (the part of the brain directly behind your forehead) effectively disconnects. Unfortunately, the prefrontal cortex is the part of the brain responsible for logical, rational thought and problem solving. When you're angry, you are left with only your emotional responses and physical reactions, a condition known to most parents as "losing it." Brain researchers sometimes call this "taking the low road." Your son, no matter what age he is, can lose it, too. And when both of you have lost it, solving problems and remaining connected is all but impossible.

Getting Back on the High Road

All parents lose their tempers from time to time. One of the greatest challenges in providing discipline for your son is learning to manage your own emotions wisely. When you lose it, it is always best to take a moment or two to calm yourself down. You can take deep breaths, throw cold water in your face, or talk to a friend. When you have reconnected to yourself, you will be better able to be kind and firm with your son.

Your son needs to learn to reconnect, too. Time-out is most effective when it is used as a cool-off, an opportunity for your son to calm down. A positive time-out is a wise first step in solving problems together when emotions run high.

Invite your son to help you create a cool-off spot somewhere in your home; supply it with items that will help him calm down, such as soft toys, music or story tapes, or drawing supplies. When your son loses his temper, remember that before he can solve problems, he needs to reconnect. You can say, "Looks like you're pretty mad at me. Why don't you go to your cool-off spot? When you feel better, we'll talk about this problem." You can even offer to go with him.

Fact

When human beings become angry, we revert to the most primitive parts of our brain. Some scientists call this the reptile brain. When you and your son lose your tempers, you might as well be *Tyrannosaurus rexes* shrieking and clawing at one another. It is always best to cool off and become human again before attempting to resolve an argument.

Older boys can often cool down by listening to music, shooting baskets, or calling a friend. Remind yourself that you are not letting your son off the hook; instead, you are teaching him self-awareness and self-control so that he can then solve problems more effectively.

Teaching Life Skills

Parents do a great many things in the name of self-esteem. They praise their children, they get children involved in sports and activities, they buy their children name-brand clothing and popular toys, and they often sacrifice their own needs so their children will have what they want. What researchers tell us, however, is that none of these things will give children self-esteem. In fact, you cannot give your son self-esteem at all; he must grow it for himself. The best way to accomplish this important task is by teaching your son life skills.

Think about a time when you tried something new, faced a challenge, or took on a task you weren't sure you could accomplish—and you succeeded. How did you feel? Chances are you felt proud, confident, and optimistic. Learning skills and mastering a challenge—

what experts call competency experiences—are vital to developing healthy self-esteem. When parents do too much, children never get the opportunity to learn about their own capability and resources. They never get the chance to build their own self-esteem.

Your son should participate in the daily tasks of making a family work. But rather than assigning him chores, consider inviting him to learn skills. When your son knows how to do things for himself, he will develop confidence, which in turn will help him resist unhealthy peer pressure. Your son will also develop a sense of belonging and significance when he knows he is a contributing member of his family.

There are many ways to teach your son life skills. For starters, you can invite your son to keep you company as you work in the home or yard. Let him try his hand at tasks; remember, you must teach him the skills involved in doing a job well. Consider his age; a teenager can mow the lawn easily while an eight-year-old may feel discouraged. Be sure to say thank you when he helps you.

You must also allow your son to try—and sometimes fail. Your boy will not be damaged by failure; in fact, he can learn courage and coping skills when you allow him to try without rescuing him. Stay close and offer support, celebrate when he succeeds, and offer empathy when he fails.

 Essential

Be sure to offer encouragement. Praise is usually given when someone succeeds at a task; encouragement notices the small steps along the way. Make sure your son knows that you see him trying; encourage his efforts in the right direction even when he falls short of his goal.

Perhaps most importantly, you must teach your son to build on his strengths and to manage his weaknesses. Everyone is not gifted at the same things. Your son may be a natural athlete or a talented student; he may love computers or music. Whatever he loves, give him opportunities to enjoy it. When your son must do things he dislikes, avoid blame and shame and look instead for solutions. Remember, mistakes are opportunities to learn.

Discipline is about far more than responding to misbehavior. Effective discipline—teaching your son character, attitudes, and skills—is something that should happen every hour and every day of your lives together. At its heart, discipline is a powerful expression of your love for your son.

CHAPTER 7

Boys and Emotions

There are a number of differences between boys and girls, especially early in life. Despite the fact that boys are often more emotionally sensitive and develop social and emotional skills more slowly than do girls, the emotional wiring in male and female brains is essentially the same. Yet in most cultures (and in many families), parents still believe that while girls should be able to cry, to giggle, and to be afraid, boys should not.

The Myth of the Stoic Male

Imagine a man named Gary, who, although he is now thirty-eight years old, still remembers how it felt to be nine. "My parents were both fabulous athletes," he recalls. "They ran marathons and played tennis. They were used to overcoming pain, and they thought I should, too. So when I hurt myself or felt sad, their response was always the same: 'Suck it up.'" Gary shakes his head. "I still struggle with the idea that my own son has feelings, and that it's okay." In his book *Real Boys: Rescuing Our Sons from the Myths of Boyhood*, William Pollack, Ph.D., describes what he calls the Boy Code, the culturally ingrained code of acceptable behavior that dictates what boys can feel— and what they cannot. This code leads boys to say they are okay when they are not, to avoid asking for help, and to run from any appearance of softness or weakness.

Writes Dr. Pollack, "The Boy Code is so strong, yet so subtle, in its influence that boys may not even know they are living their lives in accordance with it. In fact, they may not realize there is such a thing until they violate the code in some way or try to ignore it. When they do, however, society tends to let them know—swiftly and forcefully—in the form of a taunt by a sibling, a rebuke by a parent or a teacher, or ostracism by classmates."

Think about the last time you saw a boy get hurt at a baseball or soccer game. Mothers do not rush onto the field; even fathers often hang back, letting the coaches handle the matter. When a boy rises and limps off the field of combat, the spectators applaud and cheer. The message is clear: Boys should not show pain or fear. Boys must keep going even when they're hurt.

 **Fact**

The world is not kind to men who show emotion. Consider the political career of Edmund Muskie. During the 1972 presidential campaign, Muskie cried while responding to criticism of his wife; his tears essentially ended his political career. In 2004, Howard Dean's presidential campaign faltered when he became so excited that he screamed in jubilation.

As it turns out, boys have the same range of emotions wired into their brains as girls do. What accounts for the different beliefs we have about boys, girls, and emotion?

The Voice of Culture

Most human societies throughout history have been patriarchal. That is, men run the government, own the property, and assume responsibility for providing for women and children. Many religions bolster the notion that men are inherently more responsible and reliable, while women are relegated to a secondary position, keeping the home and raising the children. In earlier times, the very survival of a community and its families depended on a man's strength—his ability to hunt, to farm, and to provide shelter and security for those in his care.

Few families these days depend on Dad to hunt down dinner, but some of those early cultural beliefs about gender remain. Among the strongest are the notions we hold about men and women, boys and girls, and what they should (or should not) feel.

The Purpose of Emotions

You may remember *Star Trek*, the 1960s classic television program. One of the leading characters on that program, Mr. Spock, came from a race that felt no emotions. Spock operated on pure logic; his decisions were dictated by reason rather than messy, unreliable emotions. Many adults long for a similarly uncluttered way of life. But the truth is that emotion is vital to human existence, and managing emotions well is a significant part of being healthy and happy.

Researchers have believed for some time that emotion (rather than logic) is the driving force in the human brain. Recent studies show that emotion may actually be the link that connects the various functions of the brain and helps them work together. In other words, emotion integrates the different parts of the brain.

 **Essential**

Emotions are the data you need to make decisions and to stay safe. When you feel lonely, you need companionship. When you are afraid, you need to protect yourself. If you are aware of your emotions and learn to pay attention to them, you will always know how to take care of yourself.

Some researchers tell us that emotion ties together physiological, cognitive, sensory, and social processes, allowing our bodies, thoughts, and senses to work together. Rather than being messy, sissy feelings that complicate our lives (best kept private or stuffed away altogether), emotions actually may be responsible for neural integration, keeping us sane, healthy, and functioning effectively. Emotion appears to be the linking force that allows the different parts of our brain to talk to each other.

It is all the more tragic, then, that our culture effectively discourages boys from understanding and feeling their emotions. Numerous writers and researchers, among them Michael Thompson, Dan Kindlon, Terrence Real, William Pollack, and Michael Gurian, have noted the silent crisis that occurs when boys lose the ability to connect with their feelings. Boys are at greater risk for depression, suicide, academic problems, and drug and alcohol abuse than are girls, often because they not only lack the ability to understand and learn from their emotions, they actively suppress them. If emotion is intended by nature to keep your son healthy, how can you teach him to understand his feelings, to manage them effectively, and to behave with thoughtfulness and flexibility in a world that does not make a boy's emotional journey easy?

Teaching an Emotional Vocabulary

All too often, boys learn that the ideal man is the strong, silent type. He looks like Arnold Schwarzenegger or Bruce Willis (Clint Eastwood or John Wayne for an older generation) and mutters phrases like "I'll be back," "Make my day," or "Bring it on." Weak men are "girly men." Many boys have exactly two speeds when it comes to emotion: They are "okay," or they are "angry." Many parents are shocked at how quickly their sons become belligerent, but it should come as no surprise. Anger is culturally acceptable for boys (and men) and creates its own set of problems. (You will learn more about boys and anger later on.)

In *I Don't Want to Talk about It: Overcoming the Secret Legacy of Male Depression*, psychotherapist Terrence Real, L.I.C.S.W., talks about the emotional numbing that boys experience as they grow up. They begin life as exuberant, lively little people with a full range of feelings, but by the time they have spent some time in school, they have discovered what "real men" are like and have begun to restrict their expressiveness. Research shows that most males struggle not only to express, but to identify their emotions. The formal term for this difficulty is *alexithymia* and psychologist Ron Levant, Ed.D., M.B.A., estimates that as many as 80 percent of men in our society have a mild to severe form of it. If you ask most men what they are feeling, you are likely to hear what they are *thinking* instead. Men (and their sons) often find it difficult to tell the difference.

Alert!

Perhaps the most devastating emotion young boys experience as they grow up is shame. No one enjoys shame, but boys may actually fear it. Shame strikes at a boy's heart; it causes him to close down and to avoid connection with adults at the very time he needs it most. Discipline for your son should never involve humiliation or shame.

Building Emotional Literacy

Boys are healthier and happier when they have solid emotional resources and access to all of the varied and intricate parts of themselves. How can parents teach boys to have a rich emotional life, deep connections to others, and still be full members in the society of men?

To build emotional literacy in your son, you should start by teaching your son an emotional vocabulary. From the time your son is an infant, speak to him with a rich and varied emotional vocabulary. Babies are not born with words for their feelings; they must be taught. You can say, "You look sad" or "You must feel disappointed" without rescuing or coddling your son. You can also talk about your own feelings without making your son responsible for them. When you can say, "I felt scared; did you?" to your boy, you give him permission to feel and to express his own emotions.

Be sure to listen to your son. Then listen some more. One of the best ways to encourage expression is simply to listen without judgment. Show empathy; don't rush to offer solutions. Give your son time to explore his emotions. Remember, you don't have to agree with your son's feelings to listen, nor do you have to accept inappropriate behavior. Listening well is the first step to creating connection and solving problems together.

 **Essential**

You must be sure to model connection and empathy for your son. Mothers and fathers can demonstrate by their own actions what real love and connection look like. When your son lives with respect, love, and empathy, he will find it easier to practice those skills himself.

In addition to listening and teaching your son an emotional vocabulary, make room for your son to be himself. Avoid telling your son what he should or should not feel; give him room to explore his strengths and weaknesses in a safe environment. When your son doesn't need to fear shame or rejection, he can express his emotions, needs, and dreams openly.

Remembering Your Role

Importantly, you should recognize that the outside world will "toughen up" your boy; your job is to nurture and encourage him. All boys inevitably learn the hard lessons about being a "real man." You can best help your son by nurturing his heart and spirit and providing compassion when the world hurts him.

Because boys are sometimes prone to anger and aggression, it is wise to model being calm and respectful when dealing with problems. Take a cool-off if you must, but avoid yelling and anger, and remember that emotions are not mysterious forces that threaten to overwhelm us; they are part of what makes us most human. When you can teach your boy to understand and express his feelings respectfully and clearly, you are helping him take a giant step toward true manhood.

Learning Maturity

You may be wondering whether all this emotional expressiveness will affect your son's behavior. After all, if he is too emotional, how will he control his actions? During the preschool years, their innate impulsiveness and lack of emotional skills often causes boys to act out their feelings. If they're angry, they hit someone. If they're frustrated, they stomp their feet. And if they're happy, they may leap with joy. As boys grow, however, parents can help them learn to separate their feelings from their actions. Of course, it helps if you know how to do this first.

Choosing Appropriate Behavior

It may surprise you to learn that emotional awareness actually improves your ability to behave responsibly. If you know that you are angry, for example, you can choose to do things that calm you; you can talk about your anger and look for solutions rather than directing your anger at someone else. If you are worried, you can choose actions that help you solve your problems, rather than hiding from them, medicating them, or making them worse.

Simply put, what you *feel* can (and often should) be different than what you *do*. You can learn to identify your feelings (putting a hand over your heart and taking a few deep, calming breaths is a good place to begin), and then decide what you want to have happen. You may say, "I'm really angry at you right now. I need a moment to calm down, and then we can figure out how to solve this problem." Expressing emotions respectfully and calmly is always better than acting them out.

Emotional Maturity

You can teach your son these same emotional management skills. He, like you, can learn that feelings need not dictate behavior, but that he can make better choices when he understands his own emotions *and* thinks about how to act in response. For instance, you might say to him, "You seem pretty worried about your math test. What things can you think of to help you get ready?"

A wise old soldier once said that courage is not the absence of fear; it is feeling the fear and doing what must be done in spite of it. Emotional maturity means having emotional awareness *and* choosing to act in helpful ways. It's wise to recognize that it will take your son years of practice to master this important life skill.

Anger: *The Acceptable Male Emotion*

Stand on any school playground and watch what happens around you. You'll see groups of children playing, some children wandering by themselves, and occasionally, children arguing and fighting. And depending on whether those children are girls or boys, you will notice differences in how they express their anger. The boys may argue, have fistfights, or throw things at each other. The girls usually sulk, pout, or spread gossip.

Boys and Anger

Anger has long been an acceptable emotion in boys and men. After all, the reasoning goes, they have lots of testosterone; they can't help being aggressive. Indeed, anger, including fistfights or other physical confrontations, is often seen as true masculine behavior. Even in these supposedly enlightened times, someone who walks away from a fight may be called a coward.

Numerous studies have shown that there is no real difference in the way men and women *experience* anger. All people feel anger, and most feel angry about the same things. However, men and women (and boys and girls) *express* their anger in different ways. Men tend to be more physically aggressive, to engage in passive-aggressive behavior more often, and to be more impulsive in expressing anger. Women stay angry longer, are more resentful, and often use relationships as weapons in expressing anger (such as excluding a former friend, starting unpleasant rumors, or insulting someone's appearance).

Question?

My nine-year-old son is being bullied. When he asks for help from teachers, the other kids tease him. What can I do?
Your son will have to decide what he must do to make his way in the world of his peers. Boys this age do not yet respect quiet strength and gentleness; be willing to listen to your son and offer him unconditional love and support.

Some experts believe that boys are prone to anger because it is an emotional substitute for other, less acceptable emotions, such as sadness or loneliness. Parents, too, contribute to boys' anger; research has shown that parents encourage daughters to resolve conflicts peacefully but allow boys to retaliate. Anger is a normal part of the human emotional spectrum; in fact, anger is often what motivates us to solve problems, to stand up for ourselves, and to attempt to right the wrongs of the world. Misdirected anger, however, can cause great harm.

Managing Anger

Everyone gets angry from time to time; your son will, too. How you respond to his anger will teach him about how to recognize and manage it as he grows. First, though, you must learn to deal with your own anger effectively. If you yell, scream, and throw things, your son will, too. Admit your own strong feelings, take a time-out when necessary, and focus on solving problems rather than spreading blame.

You must then teach your son that anger is acceptable, but hurting people or things is not. You can help your son learn that he can feel angry without hurting himself or someone else. Accept his anger and offer him ways to cool down when he needs them. Then, when everyone is calm, sit down and explore ways to make the situation better.

One option you could explore when teaching your son how to deal with anger is to create an anger wheel of choice with your son. Sometime when you are both calm, make a pie chart with suggestions for things he can do when he is angry. Options might include taking a time-out, listening to music, calling a friend, or shooting baskets in the backyard. Then, when your son is upset, he can look at the wheel of choice for ideas. Having solutions already at hand will help him calm down more quickly.

Finally, learn to listen to your son's real feelings and help him find words to express them. Your son's body language, facial expressions, and gestures will help you know what he is feeling. Gently help him find the right words for his emotions before he reaches the boiling point. Anger is often a smoke screen for other, more difficult feelings; when your son can talk about these feelings openly with you, anger may be unnecessary.

Remember, most boys fight, argue, sulk, and suffer. And most boys get up to live and fight another day. Remain calm, remember that feelings are just feelings, and do your best to find solutions to the everyday challenges life with your son presents.

Boys and Depression

Depression has become an easy word to toss around. These days, almost anyone who is feeling a little down can claim to be depressed. Still, depression is a clinical term and like it or not, far too many boys suffer from serious depression, especially during adolescence. Depressed boys may be hard to spot; they don't always sulk in their rooms, looking sad and lonely. Depression in boys often takes the form of rage, extreme irritability, or drug and alcohol use. Depressed boys may avoid school, stop doing their work, and become increasingly disconnected from parents and friends. They may even begin to talk about suicide.

Alert!

Every year there are an average of 1,890 suicides among fifteen- to nineteen-year-olds; 1,625 of them are committed by boys. Girls attempt suicide more often, but boys' attempts are more lethal, often because boys have been unable to express sadness and isolation. Parents must keep a strong connection with boys and should not hesitate to get professional help when needed.

Many experts believe that boys' susceptibility to depression stems from the lack of connection they often feel with parents and other adults. Grief and loss, such as a death or the divorce of parents, can also trigger depression.

The best way to prevent depression and other emotional problems is to stay connected, to listen, and to spend time just being together. Sometimes, though, boys suffer depression despite the best efforts of their parents. How can you tell if your son is struggling with depression? Keep an eye out for the following behaviors that could be signs of depression:

- **Frequent, angry outbursts or impulsive behavior.** All boys have a bad mood now and then, but depression often leads boys to become increasingly hostile and filled with rage.
- **Lack of interest in activities and friends he used to enjoy.** He may appear bored, exhausted, or listless and may be "too tired" to participate in sports or other activities. He may also argue with friends more often, or report that he has no friends.
- **Changes in sleep patterns, eating, or weight.** He may sleep all the time or tell you he can't sleep at all. He may report that

he's not hungry when he hasn't eaten a solid meal for days.

- **Low self-esteem.** He may express harsh criticism of himself, see only his failures, and lose confidence in his ability to succeed at a task.
- **Increased risky behaviors.** A depressed boy may begin taking unnecessary chances; teenagers may drive too fast, drink too much too often, or experiment with drugs.
- **Difficulty with academic work.** He may lose interest in school work, skip classes, refuse to do homework, and bring home lower grades.

It's important to note that none of these symptoms alone means your son is depressed or at risk for suicide. However, if you begin to notice several of these signals, or any other marked change in your son's mood or behavior, it is wise to pay attention and to make an extra effort to draw him out. If you are concerned about your son's emotional health, don't hesitate to find a skilled therapist who can work with your son to help him resolve these issues. Depression isn't weakness; it can be healed with time and care.

Keeping Your Son Connected

Too many boys lack the emotional awareness and resiliency they need to live happy and successful lives. You may have been more concerned about your son's grades and behavior than his emotional health, but your son depends on you to keep him connected, to teach him emotional literacy, and to help him identify and express his feelings. Emotions are not just for girls. All healthy human beings have them and must learn to manage them effectively.

You may worry that teaching your son emotional awareness and talking openly about feelings may make him too soft to survive in the world. In truth, adding the language of emotion to your lives together can only make him stronger. You can honor his pride and his innate boyness at the same time that you teach him to be connected to his inner self and to those around him.

Your son may hesitate to talk openly about feelings, but he probably won't mind being asked for help in solving problems. You can learn a great deal about the way he sees the world by inviting his opinion on issues and challenges you face together. What does he think about his friends' behavior? What would make his school a better place? Is there a way to make household chores fairer for everyone? It is in the context of these everyday topics that you can connect with your boy.

Your son will need your help to develop courage, to learn to be the best boy—and eventually, the best man—he can be. Accept all the parts of your son, his strengths and weaknesses, his thoughts and emotions. Love and awareness will help you keep him whole and guide him toward a healthy, successful life.

CHAPTER 8

Boys and Dads

Throughout the centuries, art, literature, and popular culture have explored the special relationship between boys and their fathers. From Abraham and Isaac in the Old Testament to Ward Cleaver, the Beaver, and Wally in television's *Leave It to Beaver,* fathers and sons have enjoyed a close and sometimes complicated connection. Many men spend a lifetime longing for a father's love and approval. How can you as a father create a secure, loving relationship with your son?

What Sons Learn from Their Fathers

Fathers are different from mothers. They look different, they sound different, they play in a different way, and they usually have a different approach to raising children than a mother does. And that's a good thing. A boy learns from his father, without even realizing he's doing it, what a man is and does. He learns about masculinity, about what men like and don't like. Many adult men report that they either wanted to be "just like my dad"—or wanted to be his exact opposite. Fathers undoubtedly have a powerful influence on their growing sons, and it begins from the moment of birth.

Fatherhood in the Early Years

Imagine a couple who have just welcomed the birth of a son. Curt was thrilled when his wife Nancy announced that she was pregnant with their first child.

He was even more excited when tests showed that the baby was a boy. Curt had wonderful memories of camping trips and fishing expeditions with his own dad, and he looked forward to giving his son a happy and loving childhood. He attended childbirth classes enthusiastically, listened to parenting books on tape as he drove to work each day, and was right beside Nancy when she gave birth to Alex.

Once Alex was at home, though, Curt began to feel unsure of how to behave. Alex was so *small*. Nancy nursed him and seemed to know just how to handle his burps, cries, and various physical needs. Curt loved watching his wife hold Alex and care for him; Nancy laughed and said they'd need to build an extra room to store the photos Curt was taking. But when it came time for Curt to hold Alex, to feed him, or to bathe him, he felt clumsy and insecure. The baby seemed to be his mom's territory, and suddenly those camping trips seemed a long time away.

Challenges for Dads

Fathers sometimes find their sons' infancy challenging. They love the baby and delight in his noises and new activities, but infant care seems to be Mom's province. Devoted mothers sometimes unwittingly prevent Dad from taking a more active role by insisting that the baby be held, fed, and rocked in a particular way (usually hers). Dads often disappear, falling back on work and providing for their new family. Sometimes they don't reappear for years, if at all.

A father's role in the raising of his children has changed dramatically over the past century or two. In generations past, sons expected to follow in their fathers' footsteps, apprenticing in their work and in their approach to life. During the nineteenth century, however, fathers began to go out to work, and the measure of a man's success slowly changed. Rather than the closeness of his family and the strength of his family business, a man's worth could be measured in his income, the value of his house, and the size of his car. Parenting became "women's work"; fathers were just too busy earning a living. And generations of boys grew up hungering for closeness with a father they barely knew, someone who came home only to eat dinner, look over homework, hear about the day's misbehavior, and watch a little television.

 **Fact**

Ross Parke, Ph.D., at the University of California at Riverside, found that fathers are just as good at reading a baby's emotional cues as mothers are, but they respond in different ways. A father's active play and stimulation may actually help a baby learn to be aware of his own internal state and to tolerate a wide range of people and activities.

Research shows that without a doubt, fathers are an integral part of their sons' healthy emotional, physical, and cognitive growth from their first moments of life. Boys whose fathers love them and can demonstrate that love in consistent, caring ways have fewer problems later in life with peers, academics, and delinquent behavior. One study tracked a group of boys and girls for twenty-six years, exploring the roles of both mothers and fathers in nurturing emotional health and empathy. While the mother's role was important, by far the most influential factor in a child's emotional health was how involved the *father* was in a child's care. In fact, the benefits of having an active, involved father during infancy and early childhood appear to last well into adolescence.

Critical Dads, Hungry Sons

Sadly, many loving fathers never learn to communicate love in ways their boys can hear and feel. Think of this scenario: Paul was six years old when his mom and dad divorced. Paul had a close and loving relationship with his mom, but he adored his dad. They spent hours digging in the garden, watching basketball, and hitting baseballs together. Paul's parents worked hard at minimizing the effect of their divorce on their only son. Paul spent an equal amount of time with both parents, and his dad came to Scouts and to all of his soccer and tee-ball games.

Over time, though, things began to change. Paul's dad remarried, and his new wife found Paul's presence an inconvenience. Paul's dad began to appear less often at his games and school programs. Paul was a gifted student and a hardworking athlete, but his dad began to find fault with his accomplishments. No matter how hard Paul tried, his dad seemed to think he could have done more. He became so critical and demanding that even Paul's stepmother began to notice and to tell her husband to "take it easy on Paul."

Essential

As boys reach adolescence, their inborn drive to individuate, to become independent people, may lead them to compete and argue with their fathers. Fathers often react by trying to control their sons' opinions and actions, causing conflict. As your boy grows, remember, he is becoming himself and needs your support and understanding.

By the time he was in high school, Paul began to avoid spending time at his dad's house, eventually choosing not to spend the night there. He airily told his worried mom that it didn't bother him, but secretly his dad's distance and disapproval broke his heart. Paul's grades remained good, he was never in trouble, and he had solid friendships with good young men. He even convinced himself that his dad's constant criticism was a sign of love. Still, there was an empty spot in Paul's heart. Deep down, he longed for his dad to be proud of him.

Chances are that Paul was right—his father certainly loved him. But fathers don't always know how to connect with their sons. As

Dan Kindlon, Ph.D., and Michael Thompson, Ph.D., report in *Raising Cain*, ". . .they find it difficult to think in terms of 'love' or to express the love they do feel for a son. Instead, they tend to fall back on what they have been taught to do with other men—namely, compete, control, and criticize."

In a recent study, male executives and managers were asked what single thing they would have changed about their childhood relationships with their fathers. Most of these successful men answered that they wished they had enjoyed a closer relationship with their fathers, and that their dads had been able to express more warmth and emotion.

Play and Active Love

Many truly loving dads feel a bit uneasy about showing affection to their young sons. Moms are usually comfortable hugging and cuddling, but fathers, who may never have enjoyed an openly loving relationship with their own fathers (and may not be emotionally literate themselves), often hesitate to show affection and warmth in overt, physical ways. Love need not be expressed only in the verbal, huggykissy ways that moms choose. There are many ways a father can demonstrate his love for his son, and it's important that he do so as often as possible.

Take Time to Play

Spending time together just listening, laughing, and hanging out may be one of the best ways to build a strong bond with your growing son. You can crawl around on the floor with the farm animals and cars when he's a toddler; you can build castles out of blocks or teach him your favorite sport as he grows. You can wrestle, tickle, bounce, and run. And when your son is a teenager, you can share your passion for rebuilding classic cars, fly fishing, or almost anything else. You can certainly invite your son to share the activities you enjoy, but take time to notice what *he* loves, and find ways to join in with him. You may talk and laugh; you may do some serious listening. But you will be able to connect just by sharing the same space for a while.

Of course, for busy fathers with many responsibilities, finding "hang-out time" can be a challenge. If you consider that your presence in your son's life increases his chances of being successful and happy, you may well decide that there is no higher priority.

Alert!

It's wonderful to share activities with your boy. Be careful, however, that you don't turn those shared times into unwanted lessons and lectures. Allow your son to learn at his own pace; focus on your relationship with him rather than how well he is performing a certain task. Encouragement and connection will earn you a companion for life.

Dads and Nonverbal Love

There is another way that fathers can connect and show warmth and caring to their sons, a way that requires no words at all. Imagine Sam, who is the father of an eleven-year-old boy named Brad. Sam was in the kitchen fixing a snack when Brad came through the front door. Brad's eyes were lowered, and he seemed to be barely dragging himself along. When he reached the comfortable old sofa in the den, he simply fell onto it, closed his eyes, and threw an arm over his face. He sighed deeply.

Sam placed a slice of cheese on a cracker. Brad had something going on this afternoon—what was it, he wondered? And then it struck him. Today was all-star try-outs for Little League. Brad's dejected appearance left his dad no doubt about the results: Sam knew Brad had been practicing hard, but there were a lot of talented kids trying out. Sam sighed and swallowed the discouragement he felt on his son's behalf. Then he put a few more slices of cheese and crackers on a plate and carried them into the den with a cold glass of lemonade.

Without a word, he placed the drink and the plate of snacks in front of Brad and sat down next to him. Brad glanced up, but the empathy in his father's face was too much for him; he went back to hiding behind his arm, while a tear slowly slid down his cheek. Sam reached out and stroked his son's forehead. He continued gently rubbing Brad's head and neck until his son sighed and sat up.

Brad took a sip of lemonade. "I didn't make the team, Dad," he said quietly. "They picked John Abbott instead of me. He's a really good hitter, though, so it's probably best for the team." Then he looked up at his father.

Sam smiled and put an arm around his son's shoulders. "I know you're disappointed, Brad. But I also know you gave it your best. I know how hard you worked for this." They sat quietly together a little while longer. When Brad straightened up again, Sam smiled. "Have a snack. Then why don't you keep me company out in the garage for a while? I could use your help with that cabinet I'm building."

 **Fact**

Many recent movies have explored the complex relationship between fathers and sons. Consider what the following movies say about boys and their dads: *Field of Dreams,* the *Star Wars* series, *This Boy's Life, The Prince of Tides, Billy Elliot, Road to Perdition,* and *Big Fish.* What makes a healthy, loving relationship? What sort of relationship creates distance and pain?

Sometimes nonverbal ways of communicating love say far more than the most eloquent words, especially to a boy. A warm gaze, gentle touch, and a plate of snacks let Brad know that his dad understood. Sometimes nonverbal expressions open the door for conversation, understanding, and problem solving. If you pay attention to your own feelings and to those of your son, you will be able to find ways to build powerful connections that can last a lifetime.

Fathers and Empathy

You may be surprised to learn that one of the earliest lessons baby boys learn about empathy comes through active play with their fathers. Experts theorize that being stimulated in this way allows a baby to be aware of both his father's emotional state ("Is he just playing?" "Is he mad?") and his own ("Am I tired of bouncing?" "Is this fun?"). Babies can learn to send signals such as crying or pulling away when they need less stimulation. And throughout a boy's life, his father can be one of his best teachers in the art of empathy and emotional connection.

Mirror, Mirror, on the Wall

Whether you know it or not, if you are a father, every moment of your life with your son is a lesson. You teach him what to do—and what not to do—every time you have a conversation, offer discipline, or spend time playing together. Interestingly enough, even boys without active fathers in their lives appear to master the concept of masculinity as they grow up. After all, their peers and the prevailing culture will take care of that. What they lack is the sort of nurturing and affection that fathers can offer—when they choose.

Our cultural stereotype of the strong, silent man can have a crippling effect on a man's ability to offer his son compassion, warmth, and tenderness. Yet that is often exactly what a boy needs from his father. Boys who do best in studies of psychological adjustment are those with warm, loving fathers, fathers who, perhaps ironically, have qualities often thought of as feminine. Boys who do worst in psychological adjustment are those whose fathers are abusive, overly harsh, or neglectful.

Know Who Your Son Is

When you're a father, it's tempting to focus on behavior, on teaching lessons, and on encouraging your son to achieve success (or at least to stay out of trouble). Certainly providing discipline, setting reasonable limits, and following through is an important part of fatherhood. No one, however, can nurture empathy and emotional literacy in your son as well as you can.

 Essential

True empathy means understanding the feelings and internal experience of another person; it involves awareness not only of what that person is doing or feeling, but who that person truly is.

One gift a father can give his son is unconditional acceptance and understanding. (This is not always easy, especially when your son turns out to have dreams very different from your own.) Another gift is the truth about your own feelings and experience. Remember, you and your son (and all human beings) have mirror neurons that enable you to read another's physical movements, emotions, and nonverbal messages. When you express your feelings clearly, simply, and in nonthreatening ways, your son has the opportunity to learn from your feelings and his own.

Simply put, your son needs calm, clear information about what you think and feel. You can say, "I'm pretty angry at you right now," instead of yelling. You can say, "I'm disappointed because I didn't get the promotion I wanted," instead of stalking off to your study alone. When you demonstrate emotional honesty and empathy, you offer your son the ability to nurture those qualities himself and to become a stronger, happier man.

How and When to Support Mom

It's no secret that even in the happiest marriages (or most peaceful divorces), moms and dads don't always agree on parenting. One parent is usually stricter, while the other is more lenient, and parents sometimes argue over who is "right" when neither is being particularly effective. In general, parents should do their best to work out their differences in private and to present a united front when dealing with the children. Sometimes, though, it's difficult for a father to know when to step back and let Mom have her way, and when to intervene.

During a little boy's infancy and childhood, mothers usually provide most of the hands-on parenting. Not surprisingly, many little boys and their moms develop a close bond, and that worries some fathers. We will explore a boy's relationship with his mother in more depth in Chapter 9, but even the most enlightened father may occasionally fear that closeness with Mom may create a boy who is tied to the apron strings or who becomes a mama's boy.

You can support your son by supporting his mother. Many fathers admit feeling a bit jealous of the closeness between a son and his mom, especially during the early years, but parenting is not a competition. (At least, it shouldn't be!) Your son benefits from the relationship he has with each of you. Here are some suggestions for supporting the connection between your boy and his mother:

- **Give your son permission to feel close to his mother and occasionally, to need her.** This may seem obvious, but some men shame their sons for needing a hug or physical comfort from their mothers. Be sure your boy knows that you understand his love for his mother and that you encourage it.
- **Stay actively involved in your son's care, from birth until he leaves your home.** Take time to learn the necessary skills, and then spend as much time as you can caring for your son physically and emotionally. If his mother objects, gently remind her that you, too, are a parent and that your son needs both of you.
- **Support your son's mother when she disciplines your son.** When parents openly disagree about discipline, children learn the fine art of manipulation. Learn all you can about discipline, and then, if you disagree with a discipline decision, talk about it in private and look together for solutions.

- **Treat your son's mother with respect.** Your son will learn how to treat women by watching you. Even when you disagree, make an effort to speak calmly and respectfully. Avoid criticizing his mother to your son.

James M. Barrie, the author of *Peter Pan*, once said, "The God to whom little boys say their prayers has a face very much like their mother." Boys want to love and feel close to both of their parents. By supporting his relationship with his mother, you will strengthen your son's relationship with you.

Being Your Son's Role Model

Think for a moment about your own father. You may not have known him well, or you may have years of precious memories. What did your father teach you about being a man? About values? About love and family? If your memories of your father are troubling ones, how would you change your own past if you had the chance?

The wonderful thing about raising a son is that it allows you both to share the best parts of your own childhood and, perhaps, to give your son the things you never had.

Work, Money, and Values

Children are always making decisions. They watch what happens around them, and then decide what they must do to find belonging and connection. Children do not automatically mimic the behavior and values of their parents; they are thinking, feeling people who must decide for themselves what works in life.

Still, your own choices, actions, and values are the plumb line that your son will use to measure what matters in life. If you work long hours, no matter what your reasons might be, your son will make decisions about work, about family, and about your priorities. If you compete with colleagues, family, and the neighbors to have the biggest house, the nicest boat, and the newest car, your son will decide whether he agrees with you—or not. If you tell your son that you value honesty, but he hears you calling in sick to go skiing or bragging about how you managed to avoid paying taxes, he will make his own decisions about ethics—and about you.

 **Fact**

> Researchers spent four years observing thirty-two families in which both parents worked and there were at least two children. These families, they discovered, were in the same room only 16 percent of the time; in five homes, family members were never in the same room. Only one father spent time with his children on a regular basis.

The best way to learn what your son is deciding about life and how to live it is to spend time listening and building a strong connection with him. Children are gifted observers; they rely far more on nonverbal messages than on words. "Do as I say, not as I do" doesn't work with children (especially with teenagers). Remember the list of qualities and character attributes that you want for your son? It's wise to stop occasionally and consider whether or not your own behavior and choices are nurturing those qualities. The good news is that mistakes aren't fatal; they are wonderful opportunities to learn.

Rupture and Repair: Dealing with Mistakes

It is inevitable. Even the most loving and committed parent loses his temper, makes poor choices, or says hurtful, shaming things. No parent enjoys hurting his child, but what truly matters is what you do *after* a blow-up has occurred. Daniel Siegel, M.D., puts it this way: "Although ruptures of various sorts may be unavoidable, being aware of them is essential before a parent can restore a collaborative, nurturing connection with the child. This reconnecting process can be called repair . . . Ruptures without repair lead to a deepening sense of disconnection between parent and child."

It is important to notice that your son is not responsible for mending the ruptures in your relationship: Repair always begins with parents. While it may not be easy to admit your own mistakes or to take responsibility for lost tempers and wrong choices, this, too, is part of being a role model for your son. He wants to know that you are capable and competent so that he can believe in his own capability and competence. But he also needs to know that it is okay to admit mistakes, to take personal responsibility, and to say "I was wrong" when it is appropriate to do so. Ruptures can actually make relationships stronger and closer *when* parent and child—father and son—learn to forgive, find solutions, and reconnect.

The Gift of Fatherhood

Michael Gurian, family therapist and author of numerous books on boys, shares an old Turkish saying, "You are not an adult until you have had a child." In many cultures, having and raising children is the mark of a mature human being, and setting aside one's personal needs and ambitions for the welfare and happiness of children is unquestioned. Says Gurian, "I studied thirty cultures and could not find a single one where children are more profoundly lonely than in America. Simultaneously, our adults seem the loneliest, too. In my studies, I found that American parents . . . were the most likely to want to absorb their child into their busy lives and the least likely to say they would give up their busy lives for their child."

No one is suggesting that you sacrifice your own life and dreams for your son. But if you take a moment to look deep inside, you may discover that your son is not the only one who craves connection; fathers do, too. Your son needs your guidance and encouragement in mastering the skills of maturity and in learning to be honest, empathic, and aware. From his first finger-painting to his first job, he will seek your approval in everything he does (whether he shows it or not). Your boy is exquisitely attuned to what you think of him—or what he *believes* you think of him. Even his misbehavior is designed to get your attention and to provoke a reaction.

But being a connected, loving father will enrich your life as well. Your son can teach you curiosity; he can show you how to appreciate the wings of a moth or the usefulness of mud. He can open your mind to new worlds and ideas, if you will let him—and if you can let go of your own beliefs and busyness for just a moment or two. Your son can teach you about wonder, imagination, and heartbreak, all in a single afternoon. The time you spend just being your son's dad may be the wisest investment you ever make, in his life and in your own.

CHAPTER 9

Boys and Moms

More than a century ago, Sigmund Freud put into words something that has since become one of the most deeply ingrained tenets of parenting boys. "[A boy's] relationship [with] the mother," he wrote, "is the first and most intense. Therefore, it must be destroyed." Was Freud right? Does it really make a boy "soft" if he is close to his mother? Loving moms must find the balance between nurturing their sons and encouraging independence and confidence.

The Dilemma of Mothers and Sons

Freud was certainly right about one thing: A little boy's relationship with his mother is usually his first experience of intimacy. She feeds him from her breast, rocks him to sleep, and appears by his crib when he cries in the night. As he learns to walk, it is usually his mother who provides the safe place from which he ventures out to explore his world and who cuddles him warmly when he returns. It is often Mom who volunteers at school, Mom who plans the birthday parties, and Mom who drives carloads of boys to soccer practice.

Yet when her son approaches adolescence, a mother begins to receive subtle signals that it's time to let go. No more public hugs; touch becomes something that must be carefully monitored. Well-meaning mothers, worried about "smothering" their growing boys, may withdraw from their sons, leaving them to the world of men and

the myths of masculinity. It is a loss—and an unnecessary one—for both mothers and sons.

Boys, too, feel pressure to put some emotional distance between themselves and their mothers. After all, who hasn't heard the dreaded epithets mama's boy, sissy, and tied to the apron strings? As you have learned, American culture places a high premium on self-sufficiency and strength in its males, discouraging emotional awareness and expression. And everyone knows that girls (and moms) are emotional; in order to find a place as a healthy man, the reasoning goes, boys must separate themselves from their mothers.

Essential

Traditional thinking has attributed boys' delinquent behavior, aggression, even homosexuality, to weak or absent fathers and dominant mothers. Boys, this reasoning says, have to compensate for these overbearing women; they become "too masculine" (or they retreat) in self-defense. Actually, boys benefit from having mothers who are both strong and nurturing—just as they need fathers who are both strong and nurturing.

Imagine Stephen, who is fourteen years old. He loves football, video games, books, and a good joke, and he shares all of these interests with his mom, Jackie. When asked, Stephen says readily that he loves his mom. She has raised him alone, and he respects and appreciates her hard work, generosity, and unfailing support for him. When they are alone, Stephen loves to sit side by side reading and to have his back scratched. He always gives her a hug before he wanders off to his room at night.

Things change when his friends come around, however. When he leaves the house these days, he restricts himself to scowling at his mom and saying gruffly, "See you later, Mom." When Jackie comes too close or tells him to be safe, he rolls his eyes at his friends. "I know it hurts her feelings. I feel bad sometimes," he says. "But it's embarrassing to say 'I love you.' She should know that by now."

Chances are that later on, when the chaos and confusion of adolescence have passed, Stephen will feel more comfortable showing affection for his mother, even when his friends are present. For now, however, like most young men, his dignity depends on keeping his distance.

Raising a son means finding the balance between opposing forces: closeness and distance, support and letting go, kindness and firmness. Mothers can certainly learn how to provide both love and structure and to teach the skills a boy will need to become mature. Love, however, is a necessary part of parenting, and the special bond that many mothers share with their sons is an asset, not a liability. Mothers can teach their boys how to love fully and freely. They offer sons their first lessons in the power of connection.

What Sons Learn from Their Mothers

Boys learn their earliest lessons about love and trust from their mothers. According to William Pollack, Ph.D., "Far from making boys weaker, the love of a mother can and does actually make boys stronger, emotionally and psychologically. Far from making boys dependent, the base of safety a loving mother can create—a connection that her son can rely on all his life—provides a boy with the courage to explore the outside world. But most important, far from making a boy act in 'girl-like' ways, a loving mother actually plays an integral role in helping a boy develop his masculinity."

The Importance of Loving Refuge

In the early years of a little boy's life, he is torn between two choices: He longs to explore, climb, jump, and run, and he needs to stay close to the adults who allow him to feel secure. In fact, when boys begin to walk and exercise some autonomy, their activity mirrors this dual need. They wander away from Mom (into the backyard, across the playground, or to the neighbor's house) and then return for a quick conversation or a hug, just to be sure she's there.

Alert!

Some mothers, absorbing cultural messages about "real masculinity," believe that they should push their sons away emotionally, often as early as the age of two or three. Your son needs connection with you all the way through adolescence. Be sensitive about invading privacy, but separating yourself from your son will do him more harm than good.

Your son will learn self-respect and confidence when you provide a loving and secure home base for him. When you can create a sense of belonging and significance for your boy, teach him life and character skills, and practice kind, firm discipline, he learns to trust, to face challenges, and to move freely into his world. When you take time to listen to him and to focus on solutions to the problems he faces, you teach him emotional awareness and good judgment. A strong and loving relationship with a good mother can help a boy learn the skills of intimacy, support him in developing respect for other women, and prepare him for a satisfying relationship someday.

Knowing When to Let Go

Even the wisest mother can find it hard to let go in appropriate ways when her son begins to exercise his independence. Your son's desire to do things for himself, from dressing himself to reading his own bedtime story to dating, can feel like a personal rejection. One of the paradoxes of parenting is that if you do your job as a mother well, your son will eventually leave you.

As your son grows, you will learn to find the balance between offering support and stepping back to let him learn from his own experiences—and his own mistakes. Clinging too tightly can create unnecessary power struggles, especially during adolescence (a rather bumpy period for even the closest mothers and sons). Teach skills and listen well and often; then have faith in your son and let go.

Connecting with Your Son

Fathers usually build relationship with their sons through active play and stimulation; they "do stuff" together. For mothers and boys, the process is a little different. The bond between a mother and son often grows out of simply spending time together. From infancy into childhood and adolescence, a good mother is just "there." Boys often say that their mom is the one person who "understands me." That understanding usually grows out of the hours spent offering undivided attention, responding to signals and cues, and providing comfort, support, and encouragement.

Self-Awareness for Moms

You may have grown up with brothers, active boys who are a part of your childhood memories. Or you may have had sisters (or no siblings at all), and boys seem like beings from another planet. You may have an intimate, loving marriage, or you may be deeply disappointed in your partner. You may even be a single mom, perhaps because men have hurt or abandoned you.

Many women are surprised to discover that their own experiences with men color their relationship with their sons. If men have caused you pain or you do not trust them, you may find it difficult to relax with your son, to enjoy him, and to allow him to be an active, normal little boy. Your attitudes will unconsciously color your son's beliefs about his own maleness, perhaps in ways that are not in his best interest—or yours.

Awareness of your own attitudes toward men and boys will help you connect more easily with your son. Whether you express them openly or not, your beliefs about men will influence your son's feelings about himself. It may be wise to seek out a skilled therapist to help you resolve your own past so that you can build a strong, loving bond with your son.

 Essential

Behaviors that make boys different from girls, such as impulsivity, risk-taking, silence, and anger, are behaviors that many mothers struggle with the most. After all, they didn't do those things when they were kids! Take time to learn all you can about boys, and your boy in particular. Understanding will help you choose your battles and set reasonable limits.

Skills for Connecting with Your Son

A boy's bond with his mother is one of the deepest, most enduring relationships he will experience in his lifetime. It should also be one of the healthiest and most supportive. Here are some suggestions for building a strong, loving connection with your boy:

- **Listen and observe.** Good mothers are willing to spend time just listening and watching. Ask curiosity questions to draw your son out; let him finish his thoughts before offering suggestions or advice.
- **Spend time just being together.** Relationships require time. You must be willing to hang out, to play, and to do things face to face with your son. Have at least fifteen minutes a day that belong just to your boy—no multitasking allowed!
- **Respond to your son's cues.** When he says, "I can do it myself, Mom!" teach the necessary skills, be sure he's safe, and then allow him to try. It is skills and experience that build self-esteem.
- **Be curious about his interests.** If your son loves an activity, sharing his enthusiasm is a wonderful way to build

connection. Watch his favorite sport with him; admire the new skateboard tricks he learns. Understanding your son's world will keep you connected.

- **Know his friends.** There is no better way to learn about your son than to watch him at play with his friends. As your son grows, welcome his friends into your home. If he can bring his life to you, he is less likely to feel the need to hide it from you.
- **Respect his privacy.** Even little boys need time to themselves. Your son may choose to play alone in his room from time to time, or to disappear into his computer or stereo headphones. You can show him that you care and still respect his need for private space.
- **Provide kind, firm discipline and don't be afraid to follow through.** "Wait 'til your father gets home" doesn't work. Learn effective discipline skills; then be willing to set limits and follow through.
- **Be sensitive about touch, especially in public.** Hugs are wonderful, but some touch may make your son uncomfortable, especially as he gets older. You may want to have a family rule that bathrooms and bedrooms (yours and his) are "private space" and cannot be entered without knocking. Respecting his needs will keep the connection between you relaxed and open.

Boys need connection with their mothers. If the outside world does not intrude, most are happy to stay close and connected for most of their growing-up years. Your knowledge of your son will help you know when he welcomes a hug and when he does not. It is a delicate balancing act, but time and love will teach you how to stay connected to your boy at the same time that you encourage him to exercise his independence.

How Close Is Too Close?

A loving mother can provide a safe, secure base from which her son ventures forth to explore his world. Sometimes, though, even the most sensitive and caring mother can have trouble letting go and allowing her son to learn self-reliance. Your relationship with your son needs to breathe; that is, there needs to be room for both of you to come together and then move gently apart. You will need time and space to care for yourself and to nurture your adult relationships; your boy will need room to become a confident, independent young man.

Making Room for Growth

Some women struggle to allow their sons to mature. They love the baby days and thoroughly enjoy caring for every physical and emotional need of their little boys. But little boys need to grow up. In *How to Turn Boys into Men Without a Man Around the House*, Richard Bromfield, Ph.D., calls these clinging mothers "babykeepers." When a mother hangs on too long, infantilizing her son and refusing to allow him to become independent, he "can fall behind his peers. He will be less able to tolerate frustration, handle responsibility, and interact socially." Babykeeping mothers may stunt their sons' healthy development by loving them too much to let go.

Truly loving your son means teaching him the skills and attitudes he needs to eventually leave you. As your son establishes a life of his own, however, you will know that you taught him to strike out on his own and become a healthy, confident young man. Independence does not mean the end of love and connection; it simply marks a new phase of your relationship with your son.

Other Relationships

As your son grows, he will develop new friendships and relationships outside your family. Some of these friendships, especially as he enters adolescence, will not include you—at least, not directly. A wise mom understands that she will not remain number one in her son's life forever. Other relationships—with friends and, perhaps, with girlfriends—will become increasingly important as your son matures.

Your ability to listen will serve you well as your son builds a life of his own. There is an old saying that if you truly love something, you must set it free. So it is with your growing boy; he will gladly stay connected to you when you can open your hand and allow him to fly on his own.

Alert!

As time passes, your son will begin to move away from you, spending time with new friends and new activities. Taking care of yourself and nurturing your own physical, emotional, and spiritual health is an essential ingredient in raising your son. He needs to know that Mom has a life so he is free to live his own.

Mom Can Play, Too

Mothers like words. Moms talk a lot, express emotions verbally, and rely on language to build connection and closeness. But boys have a different style. While you can teach your son emotional literacy, you may discover that he is most comfortable speaking the language of action. In other words, you may be able to connect best with your son by doing things with him.

To understand how to play with your son, think of Veronica, a busy mom for whom there were never enough hours in the day. Veronica's four-year-old son Clint had his own way of letting his mom know when he was feeling neglected: He misbehaved. When Veronica got too caught up in work, community activities, or household projects, Clint simply dug in his heels and refused to cooperate. A tantrum usually ensued.

One evening Veronica went looking for her son to begin his bedtime routine. Sure enough, there he was in front of the television, playing his favorite video game. He looked up at her and scowled, and then returned to his game. Veronica bit back the reprimand that sprang to her lips, choosing instead to settle onto the floor next to Clint.

"What are you playing, Clint?" she asked him.

Clint gave her a slightly suspicious look. "You have to race these cars around, and you get points for crashing them," he explained. Then he hesitated. "Do you want to play, Mom?" he asked.

"Well, I don't know how, but I can try," Veronica said, picking up a controller and frowning at the buttons.

Of course, Clint promptly whomped his mom at the car-crashing game—three straight times. Veronica gave up, laughing, and pulled Clint into her lap for a hug. "I'm terrible at that game!" she exclaimed.

"Well, I could teach you," Clint offered, looking shyly up at his mom. "Then we could play together sometimes."

Veronica recognized that her little boy was offering to share a part of his life with her. "I'd like that," she said quietly.

Sure enough, at four o'clock the next afternoon, Clint bounded into the kitchen and announced, "Mom, it's time for your video-game lesson!" Clint was delighted to be the expert for once, and Veronica discovered that while she'd never love video games, she thoroughly enjoyed the time she spent laughing and playing with her son on *his* turf.

Playing together turned out to be a marvelous way to avoid tantrums; Clint felt connected to his mom, and Veronica got to learn about her son. It was a win-win solution.

 Essential

There is a time and place for words; in fact, by using the language of feelings, mothers can help their sons learn to be more comfortable with emotions. Boys will not always want to talk, however, especially when they're hurt or sad. Sometimes, it is the silent spaces in a relationship that speak most clearly.

What your son needs most from you is the knowledge that you are there when he needs you, a safe harbor to return to in a storm. He also needs to know that you have faith in him—in his abilities, his character, and the person he is becoming. By sharing your son's activities and interests, you send him the message that you care about what he cares about. Sure, you may not be able to join the football team with him, but you can find ways to support his interests. Simply going for a walk, touring a museum, or even grocery shopping together can provide precious opportunities to connect.

The Other Women

Children are always making decisions. As they go through life, they have feelings and thoughts about what they see, and they make unconscious decisions about what it all means. As a mother, you are your son's most influential teacher about women. The choices you make will teach your son powerful lessons about his own relationships with women.

Mothers and Sons

Imagine that you are a spectator at a mother-son playgroup, watching the pairs of mothers and sons as they join in various activities. One mother hovers over her son, pulling him back before he can take even the smallest risk. Another mother talks to a friend in the corner, ignoring her son's pleas to "look at me, Mommy." One mother hugs her son every few minutes, while he squirms and struggles to break free. Yet another follows her son around the room, picking up toys, handing him snacks, and making sure he doesn't need to do anything for himself.

All of these boys are making decisions about themselves, about their mothers, and about what they must do to belong and feel valued. They are also learning compelling lessons about women. Take a moment to think: If you wait on your son, clean up after him, and teach him that he is the center of the universe, what is he learning about women? If you insist that your son listen to your problems, carry your emotional burdens, and tell you that you look pretty, what is he learning about women? If you sleep with your son until he's well past toddlerhood, touch him constantly, and expect him to spend all of his time with you, what is he learning about women?

Respect Your Son, Respect Yourself

Perhaps the best way to create a healthy relationship with your son is to practice mutual respect. You should respect your son's individuality, his feelings, and his needs, even when you don't agree with them (or when you need to provide discipline). You should also show respect for yourself. Remember, pampering and permissiveness are not effective parenting styles; your son needs limits and boundaries to become a healthy young adult. When you offer respect to your son and also treat yourself with respect, your son is more likely to respect all of the women he encounters, from his first-grade teacher to his future wife.

Love and Courage

Boys need their mothers' love. They also need the freedom to begin their own journey through life. Mothers are parents, first and foremost, and the information in this book will help you decide how best to raise your son. But mothers also share something very special with their growing boys. No matter how much time may stretch and bend your relationship with your son, and despite the occasional arguments and silences, your son yearns for your unconditional love and support. He can step into his own life with courage when he carries your love forever in his heart.

CHAPTER 10

Preparing Your Son to Learn

E very parent remembers a boy's first day of school. He dresses carefully in new clothes and packs his supplies in his bright new backpack. Then off he goes to his classroom, ready to embark on the voyage of learning. School should be a wonderful experience, yet for many boys it is anything but. Their enthusiasm fades in the light of academic and behavior problems and unsympathetic teachers. There are a number of reasons why so many boys hate school, and ways that parents can help.

Why Boys Struggle with School

The statistics are sobering. According to the United States Department of Education, boys have consistently scored worse than girls in reading for thirty years—all ages, in every year. Two-thirds of special education students in high school are boys, and boys are 50 percent more likely to be held back in the eighth grade than girls. Boys are more likely to be diagnosed with attention deficit disorder or a learning disability; they are far more likely than girls to be referred to a school psychologist. Underneath these statistics are real flesh-and-blood boys who dread school, spend hours in the principal's office, refuse to do their homework, and tell worried parents that "the teacher doesn't like me." Why?

It's Tough to Be a Boy

Imagine this scenario: It's time for art projects at the neighborhood preschool. Fifteen four-year-olds are gathered in clusters while Mrs. Grant, the teacher, explains what to do. The girls calmly put on their plastic aprons and move to the art tables, talking quietly and gathering paper and brushes as they go. Some of the boys, however, appear to be on a different wavelength. Four are still in the play area, attempting to make their block tower the tallest one yet. Two of the boys are looking out the window at a passing dump truck. And three more boys have grabbed brushes from the girls and are having a duel, stabbing at each other and laughing.

 **Fact**

A boy's attitude toward school and learning begins with preschool. Unfortunately, many boys are expelled from their preschool programs because they don't get along with the teacher or their peers. Preschool expulsion rates are lowest in public and Head Start programs, apparently because teacher training and behavioral consultation are more common. Expulsion rates are highest in private and faith-based preschools.

"Boys, please settle down and join us at the art tables," Mrs. Grant says kindly, but the boys are busy with their own sort of fun. One or two eventually wander over and begin putting on their aprons, but for most of them, art is not nearly as enticing as what they're already doing. Mrs. Grant's patience disappears in the face of all this commotion; while the girls look on smugly, Mrs. Grant herds the duelists and the window-gazers into the time-out corner.

"I'll be sending a note home to your parents," she says firmly.

As you have learned, boys and girls develop differently, especially in the early years of life. Girls usually acquire language and social skills sooner, while boys tend to be more impulsive, more energetic, and less comfortable with reading and writing. For better or worse, most preschool and primary-grade teachers are women; they often find the competitive, active style of little boys difficult to manage.

Many young boys discover very early that the teacher doesn't seem to like them as well as she likes the girls, who may find it easier to sit quietly, follow directions, and do the work. Boys' problems with school begin early. According to the Yale Child Study Center's Foundation for Child Development, a child is approximately three times as likely to be expelled from preschool as from kindergarten through grade twelve, and boys are four-and-a-half times more likely to be expelled from preschool than girls. Most of these expulsions are for behavior problems, and many of these behavior problems happen when little boys act like little boys. By the time a boy reaches "real school," he already may have decided that the classroom is a place where he will feel incompetent, disliked, and unwanted.

Developmental Differences

Girls are not better than boys, and boys are not better than girls. But boys and girls certainly are different, especially in groups. A boy alone may be quite content to look at a book, do a puzzle, or focus on a task, but when boys gather together, competition and activity usually erupt. Boys just have to figure out what to *do* with other boys.

Boys' higher activity level and more competitive, hands-on approach to learning can create challenges for even the most understanding teacher, especially in today's large classes. While many boys are excellent students throughout their school years, most learn to read later than girls. Many experts believe that boys are often identified as troubled learners because of developmental differences rather than genuine academic difficulties.

Schools appear to value most highly the skills that girls excel at. And a boy who learns that he is a failure or a problem is unlikely to enjoy school. Failure in the classroom leads to the emotion boys fear above all others—shame. Shame, in turn, leads to lower self-esteem and disconnection from the school community. By the time high school rolls around, boys are at greater risk for academic problems, truancy, and dropping out altogether.

How Boys Learn

Over the years, experts have debated the relative strengths of boys and girls in the classroom. Girl advocates such as Carol Gilligan and Mary Pipher, Ph.D., have written eloquently about how girls' voices are stifled by the culture and by teachers who prefer boys. Test results and statistics, however, paint a different picture. Today, girls appear to be thriving. More girls than boys now go to college and graduate school, and girls' test scores in math and science have increased significantly in the past decade. While many boys are motivated students and high achievers, many more lose interest in education long before their college entrance exams.

 Essential

One of the most important factors in whether or not a boy succeeds in school has nothing to do with academics. It is a child's perception of whether or not the teacher likes him that influences his desire to learn. Children must feel a sense of belonging and connectedness in the classroom in order to work hard and learn well.

Boys love action. Whether it's in the front yard or on the movie screen, it is action that is engaging and exciting. (As you will learn in Chapter 14, many experts believe that television and video games have actually shortened children's attention spans and reduced their ability to succeed at school.) Unfortunately for most boys, life in the classroom is pretty dull. In fact, some experts believe that boys need as many as five recess periods each day to keep their focus on academic work. Sadly, recess is usually the first thing taken away from a boy who misbehaves or fails to complete his assignments. A boy is required to sit obediently in his seat for hours at a time, listening quietly and following instructions. Moving around the classroom is frowned upon, as are the sort of pranks and play that so many boys love.

Boys often do best with activities that are tailored to their more active approach to learning. Girls, on the other hand, may prefer to learn by observing and listening. Few teachers (and almost no school curricula) emphasize a hands-on learning style. And not surprisingly, boys often complain that school is boring.

In *Real Boys*, William Pollack, Ph.D., speaks about the need to "guy-ify" our schools, making them a more inviting place for boys: "Boys, just like girls, do best in schools that give them the chance to participate in learning activities that correspond to their personal interests and competencies, enabling them to sound their authentic voices and thrive as individuals." Every student, regardless of gender or ability, should be able to feel a sense of belonging and significance in the classroom. While school may not always be fun, it should never be humiliating, shaming, or discouraging.

Helping Your Son Succeed in School

To most parents, school is a place their son disappears into for hours at a time, re-emerging with homework, notes from the teacher, requests for cupcakes, and an occasional report card. You may be convinced that success in school is critical to your son's future, but chances are that you don't really know what happens to him there each day. To your son, however, school is where he spends most of his waking hours for months at a time. School is where he meets his friends, where he learns about the world, and where he discovers what the world thinks of him.

Parents are busy people; there is always too much to do and not enough hours in which to do it. Still, you are a critical part of your son's education, and you can make a tremendous difference in his school experience.

Get Involved

There are many steps you can take to improve your son's educational experience, perhaps the most important of which is to become an involved parent. Most schools are eager for parents who can volunteer in the classroom. If you work outside the home, finding time to volunteer can be difficult, but there is no better way to see what truly happens during your son's day. Whether or not your son has had academic or behavior problems, getting involved in the classroom, field trips, and other school activities is an effective way to tune into your boy's life at school and to see what he's really up to.

Rather than asking your son "how was school today?" ask open-ended questions about your son's day at school. Ask "What was your favorite part of the day?" "What did you do at recess?" Listen carefully to your son's answers. Pay attention to his emotional life and how he's feeling about school.

Communicate Caring

Grades are not the most important part of education. Be sure your son knows that you care about his school work, his successes, and his struggles. Avoid criticism and judgment; instead, focus on finding solutions when problems arise. Take time to notice and encourage your son's successes, no matter how small.

Another way to show your son that you care is to be your son's advocate. Many parents hesitate to approach a teacher with questions, often because their own school experience was uncomfortable. Still, your son needs to know that you are on his side. You can show respect for the teacher and still explore what is happening to your son in the classroom. Teachers are human, too. Personality conflicts arise, and sometimes mistakes are made. Attend parent-teacher conferences regularly and be sure your son's individual needs are considered.

You may even take your commitment to improving the school experience for your son a step further, by working within the system to create boy-friendly schools. Parent-teacher organizations, school boards, and other committees and groups are wonderful places to speak up for boys. Be sure your son's school is considering new curricula and teaching methods, as well as effective, nonpunitive approaches to discipline. You may be surprised at how much positive change one committed parent can create.

 **Fact**

As with so many things in life, your attitude toward school, the teacher, and education will have a strong influence on how your son feels and what he chooses to do. Getting involved and staying involved encourages your boy to do his best.

Boys and Books

The fact that boys perform lower than girls on the literacy portion of tests is a concern for many parents and educators alike. As the parent of a school-aged boy, you may find yourself in a situation similar to Linda's: Linda was curled up on the couch reading a book when her fifteen-year-old son Dustin flopped down next to her, dropping his backpack and scattering papers in the process.

"What's up, Dustin?" Linda asked, reaching over and mussing her son's hair.

"Nothing. I have a ton of reading to do tonight for English, though," Dustin grumbled.

"Is that a problem? You usually love to read," Linda asked.

Dustin sat upright, reaching into his backpack and pulling out two books. "Look at these! What sort of reading assignment is this?" he said disgustedly, handing his mother two paperback books.

Linda took a look. The books were *The Joy Luck Club* by Amy Tan and *Animal Dreams* by Barbara Kingsolver. "These are good books," Linda said slowly. "I've read them both, and I really enjoyed them."

"Yeah, but you're a *girl*." Dustin's voice rose. "These books are about girls and moms and relationships and stuff. Why can't we read about something *guys* like?" Dustin stomped off to his room, closed the door, and turned on his stereo. Linda looked down at the books in her hand. Actually, she thought to herself, her son had a point. Why *couldn't* he read something guys like?

Guys Read

Jon Scieszka, a longtime teacher, writer, and parent, believes that boys are subtly discouraged from learning to love books. Most primary-school teachers are women, and many choose books that appeal to them or that they consider literature. That may work well for the teachers and their female students, but what about the boys? Many boys bring reading material that interests them to school—motorcycle magazines, sports biographies, or graphic novels—and are told "those aren't real books."

Scieszka believes that boys will learn to love reading (which enhances their chances for success in school) when parents and teachers encourage them to read what appeals to *them*. Anything that involves words printed on a page counts. If it interests a boy, excites his imagination, or encourages him to explore, it's worth reading.

Another factor that discourages boys from loving books is that many of them have no male role models who love to read; consequently, boys may see reading as a feminine activity. Dads, this means you. Pick up a book now and then and let your son see you reading. Talk to him about what you learn; explore ideas together. Go to libraries and bookstores and find books or magazines that interest both of you.

Scieszka has created a Web site about books (*www.guysread .com*) especially for boys. At Guys Read, boys can find books recommended by other boys. There are also suggestions for parents and teachers about how to encourage literacy in boys. You and your son may be delighted to learn how many fascinating books are out there just waiting to be read.

Read, Read, Read

Reading and language skills are sometimes the most discouraging part of school for boys, but they don't have to be. You can help your son prepare for learning by making books part of your life as a family. Here are some suggestions:

- **Read out loud every day.** Reading together creates closeness and connection. It also encourages your son to begin identifying letters, words, and sounds. Reading out loud can be a wonderful part of life with your son. From *Pat the Bunny* to *Harry Potter*, read together and enter the world of imagination and ideas.

- **Become a storyteller.** Stories told aloud also encourage a love of words and may actually enhance brain development and processing skills. Change your voice for different characters; be dramatic. Sharing memories, history, and legends out loud is an effective way to spark a boy's interest in stories and words.

- **Visit libraries and bookstores.** Most libraries and bookstores have extensive children's collections, often including cozy armchairs and sofas. Attend readings and story times; try books on tape for quiet moments.

In this era of computers, Internet communication, and sophisticated graphics, books may seem outdated, even unnecessary. Still, reading, writing, and other language skills are critical to success in school, and later on, to work and career. There's another excellent reason to read with your boy that you may not have considered: It's great fun.

Attention Deficit Disorder

If you've spent much time in the company of boys, you already know that they can be busy, impulsive, easily distracted little people. An hour after they climb out of bed in the morning, every toy they own is likely to be on the living room floor, while they search for something new to do. They don't listen, much to the consternation of parents. They fidget and squirm, unable to sit still for more than the length of a cartoon show. And when they arrive in school, the notion of sitting in rows, following directions, and doing one thing at a time is unthinkable. But does that mean there is something wrong?

The Epidemic of ADD

You probably know someone who has attention deficit disorder (ADD) or whose child has been diagnosed with it. You may even have it yourself. But did you know that boys are up to nine times more likely than girls to be given this diagnosis? According to the National Institutes of Mental Health, between 3 and 5 percent of American schoolchildren have ADD, approximately 2 million of them. As many as 1 million boys take serious medication to deal with this problem.

 Essential

There is no medical test for ADD; instead, diagnosis relies on observation and identifying a certain number of important symptoms. Only a qualified professional, such as a doctor, psychologist, or trained therapist can accurately diagnose ADD. If a diagnosis is made, you can decide on treatment options, which do not always include medication.

Attention deficit disorder is a genuine disorder, which may occur with or without hyperactivity, and has a serious impact on children who have it. The American Psychiatric Association's *Diagnostic and Statistical Manual of Mental Disorders DSM-IV-TR* (the handbook used by professionals to diagnose mental and emotional problems) defines ADD as a combination of inattention and impulsivity, with or without hyperactivity. Children with ADD are often disorganized; they have trouble hanging onto their homework papers, frequently misunderstand assignments, are careless, and can't seem to finish their work on time. They often act without thinking things through and seem to have boundless physical energy, which may show up in the form of foot tapping and an inability to sit still (unless they're doing something they really enjoy). Before you decide that these symptoms sound like your son and rush him to the doctor, consider the rest of the definition.

Is the Behavior Causing Problems?

A child can only be diagnosed with ADD if these symptoms have been causing genuine problems for more than six months. A boy's inability to pay attention, fidgeting, and occasional defiant behavior must be getting him into trouble at school, at home, or with his friends. If he's not having trouble, he doesn't have ADD.

It's also important to recognize that grief, anxiety, depression, or other problems can mimic the symptoms of ADD in children, and an accurate diagnosis cannot be made until a child is about six years of age (most medications also are restricted to children older than six).

Not surprisingly, the difficulties active, normal boys encounter in traditional classrooms often lead to their diagnosis of ADD. A boy's normal development during the early years of his life can look a lot like ADD, but that doesn't mean there's anything wrong. Even well-meaning teachers, school counselors, and preschool staff members are not qualified to diagnose ADD. If you're concerned, be sure you talk to a trained professional.

If the Shoe Fits: Finding Treatment

If your son does have ADD, diagnosis and treatment will make his life at home and at school easier, allowing him to focus on his work, make solid friendships, and feel a sense of belonging in the classroom. Treatment may include medication, but take your time in making this decision. For many boys, training in social and life skills or sessions with a good therapist to help him understand his own behavior are enough.

Parents can help, too. Consider joining one of the many support groups for parents of children with ADD in your community; take a parenting class to improve your parenting skills. It may be helpful to know that kind, firm discipline and structure are immensely helpful to children with ADD. You can help your son create daily routines to get him through the day (getting up, getting to school, homework, and bedtime routines are good places to start). You can also help him find ways to organize his school books and assignments, and break tasks into small, more manageable steps.

Alert!

When children are not diagnosed appropriately, ADD can cause problems with school work, family life, and friendships, and it can lead to depression and risky behavior, especially in the adolescent years.

Remember, ADD has nothing to do with a boy's heart, soul, or intelligence. He is the son he has always been, and together you can find ways to deal with the challenges he faces.

Grades and Homework

Nobody's perfect, which means that sooner or later, even the best student will neglect his homework, forget to study for a test, or bring home an embarrassing report card. And parents, being human, lose their tempers, nag, scold, and worry that a C in sixth-grade math puts Harvard out of reach forever. In many families, grades and homework are among the most frequent causes of argument and heartache. It may be helpful to know that you can support your son's education without engaging in constant battles.

Some boys are exceptional students, motivated perfectionists who do homework without being asked, care about their grades, and work to potential in every class. But most boys view homework as a boring, annoying obstacle to doing what they *really* want. While the value of homework as an educational tool has been called into question, the fact remains that teachers expect it, grades depend on it, and students have to do it. Because homework and grades are unavoidable parts of your son's school life, it will help to have a plan.

Some Guidelines

To create a plan, you must first remember who the grades and homework actually belong to. The work (and the grades that go with it) belongs to your son, not you. Doing the assignment, gathering supplies, and turning in the papers is his responsibility. You can coach, support, and suggest, but wise parents know when to step back and let a child learn from the results of his own choices. Boys sometimes learn more from failure than from success.

Although it can be difficult at times, you must remember to be realistic about the meaning of grades. High-school grades matter; grades for the junior year of high school are especially important if your son plans to attend college. But no one ever checked the third-grade report card of a job applicant. Grades are just a way of measuring progress, not the measure of your boy's worth or potential. Don't panic or overreact if your son brings home a disappointing report card or test score. Instead, work with your son and his teacher to identify problems and find solutions.

Creating an Academic Plan

Work with your son to make a plan for homework. There is no one right way to approach homework. Sit down with your son and agree on a plan that works for both of you. You may agree that homework will be done right after school, or you may decide that he needs some time to blow off steam after hours in the classroom and will do homework after dinner. Many plans are possible, as long as you talk about them together and make an agreement. If you have a morning routine in place, be sure that gathering homework papers and books is part of that routine. (Homework doesn't count if it isn't turned in.)

Things to Avoid

Be sure not to focus only on discouraging academic events. Notice what's right as well as what needs improvement. If your son brings home a report card with four B's and one C, don't immediately point to the C and ask, "What happened here?" Be sure you offer appreciation for the work your boy does and the progress he makes. Discouraged boys rarely try their hardest.

Also, you should avoid punishment and/or rewards for school behavior and grades. Your son needs to learn to work hard because it's the right thing to do, not because you pay him five dollars for every A. Remember, punishment and rewards produce only short-term changes in behavior; long-term change requires teaching and encouragement.

Most importantly, when creating and carrying out an academic plan, you must make an effort to build on strengths and manage weaknesses. Every boy cannot excel in every subject. Ask your son what *his* goals are in school. You may agree that a C in science is acceptable and work toward A's in the subjects he truly loves. If you take away the computer he loves until he improves his English grade, you may both be disappointed in the results.

Education is crucial, especially in this era of increasingly sophisticated technology. Remember, though, that everyone has to start somewhere; it is more important for your son to learn how to learn than to memorize dates for a history exam. Keep your sense of humor close at hand and learn to be your son's mentor and advocate, and chances are good that you will both survive his school days.

CHAPTER 11
Boys and Their Peers

Parents and teachers are not the only people who will play an important role in your son's life. Your boy needs friends. He may begin with one or two, perhaps children from the neighborhood or preschool. When his school years begin, he will gravitate toward friends who share his interests. And by the time he is in high school, friends have all but eclipsed parents in importance. Understanding how a boy forms friendships (or fails to) will help you support him as he enters the world of his peers.

Development of Social Skills

Children aren't born with social skills. While your son is an infant, he is preoccupied with learning how to operate his body, building a connection with you, and finding ways to communicate. Babies are not able to recognize the pudgy figure in the mirror as "me" until they are about one year old; not surprisingly, their ability to relate to others takes a while to develop. At first, your son will simply play next to other children (and won't particularly care who they are). But as he becomes more aware (usually around the age of two or three), he will begin to experiment with relationships. Not all of these experiments turn out well.

The Laboratory of Play

Play is truly how a young child learns about his world. He explores, shakes, pokes, and pulls. He grabs and climbs. Unfortunately, when the object of all this activity is another child, scrapes, bumps, and hurt feelings can result. Young children have not yet learned how to share; the idea of playing cooperatively takes some getting used to. Young children see themselves as the central figure in their world, and making room for others takes time and practice.

Imagine Noah, who is three years old when he goes to preschool for the first time. He is an only child, so the busy, noisy world of other children is overwhelming at first. Being a curious, sociable boy, though, Noah finds ways to fit into this new environment and seems to enjoy himself there.

One day, as his father, Keith, is making dinner, Noah begins talking about his day at preschool. "I play with A-Hat," he says, proudly. Keith, not sure what he's heard, says, "Ahab? Who's that?"

Noah shakes his head impatiently. "Noooo, Dad, I said A-*Hat*. A-Hat is my friend." While Keith continues to puzzle over this odd name, Noah chatters about life on the playground and how he and A-Hat climbed the highest on the jungle gym—so high that the teacher asked them to please come down.

 *Fact*

By the age of two or three, gender differences appear in the ways children conduct their friendships. Girls often prefer one or two best friends and build intense relationships with them. Boys tend to gather groups of friends, playing less intensely with more people. Boys may express anger through physical aggression, while girls fight with snubs, rumors, and insults.

The next day, when Keith drops Noah off at preschool, the mystery is solved. "A-Hat" turns out to be a sturdy three-year-old wearing an Oakland Athletics baseball cap. His name, as it turns out, is James, and he lives just around the corner, but to Noah he remains

A-Hat—even without his cap. Not until the boys begin kindergarten at the same school does Noah finally call him James.

Throughout the years of elementary school, James and Noah build a friendship out of baseball, skateboards, and hanging out together. They occasionally fight, usually over the rules of a game or a broken toy, and sometimes they yell at one another. By the next morning, however, they are friends again. Even when Noah's family moves across town and he goes to a different high school, the boys still enjoy "chilling" together when the opportunity arises. Their circle of friends widens as the years pass, but they continue to share a special friendship.

"No One Will Play with Me!"

Some children seem to be born with the gift of charm. They make friends easily, are comfortable with new people and situations, and know just how to wriggle their way into a new group of children. Others, however, hang back, cling to parents, and struggle to gain admittance to games and conversations. It is heartbreaking to watch a child sit all alone or to hear him say sadly, "Nobody likes me."

A child's success in the world of his peers depends in part on his ability to send and receive accurate nonverbal signals. For instance, a child who stands too close to others, talks too loudly, dresses strangely, or touches too often will find it difficult to fit in. Other children appear angry when they don't intend to or do not know how to join a game already in progress.

 Essential

Researchers now believe that shyness may be genetically influenced; in other words, some people are shy for life. Rather than pushing your child to do something he finds difficult or discouraging, accept his temperament, focus on teaching him coping skills, and be patient as he learns.

The good news about social skills is that they can be taught—and learned. If you can, find an opportunity to observe your boy with other children and see what happens. Preschool staff and teachers may also be able to keep a kind eye on your son and let you know why he is struggling to make friends. Kind, gentle encouragement and opportunities to practice will often solve the problem.

Boys and Their Friends

Boys, like girls, crave connection and belonging. Like all of us, boys need friends, suffer when they don't believe they have any, and agonize over the ups and downs of relationships. Many adults believe that somehow boys need friends less than girls do; the myth of the stoic male has intruded even into childhood. In truth, though, no boy is an island; boys value their friends throughout childhood and adolescence and are happier and healthier when they have solid relationships with peers.

Action, Not Words

The differences in friendships between girls and boys is evident when you watch children interacting with each other. Imagine Amy and Sarah, who are best friends. They walk to school together each morning, sit on the same bench at recess, hug each other often, and always eat lunch together. While they sometimes play tetherball or do flips on the jungle gym, most of the time their heads are close together, and they are talking. They talk about everything and seem never to run out of conversation.

Jason and Lee are best friends, too—along with Adam, Rico, and Hunter. Jason talks sometimes with Lee about his parents' divorce because he knows that Lee's parents are divorced, too. But they talk in private; when the other guys are around, they play dodge ball or act out their favorite movie scenes. They would never touch each other, aside from the occasional jab or shove.

Despite the common belief that girls are better at relationships, most boys consider their friends a vital part of their lives. Boys may actually be better at maintaining friendships than girls are; a recent study of ten- to fifteen-year-old boys and girls found that girls' friendships are actually more fragile. Girls tend to say and do hurtful things to each other more frequently than boys, and girls are more hurt by the end of a friendship.

Alert!

Parents rarely object when a daughter grabs a squirt gun and pretends to be a police officer. When a boy wants to dress a Barbie doll, however, parents may worry. It is normal for young children to play with all sorts of toys and to try on the opposite gender's roles to see how they fit.

Boys' friendships are usually built around active play. Boys are the living definition of the phrase "peer group"; they love games with rules, competition, and doing things together. Boys' play usually includes a fair amount of teasing, some of which can occasionally veer off into meanness, especially if they perceive another boy as weak or clumsy. Boys seem to enjoy, even need the opportunity to test themselves against others, and many lasting friendships begin in karate class or on the basketball court. Competence and skill are widely respected; being picked last for a team or left out altogether is an experience that can haunt a boy for years.

Teens and Friendship

As boys mature, friendships become even more important, and they frequently widen to include girls. During the teen years, friends can become the most important part of a boy's life—and a part from which he excludes his parents. You will learn more about adolescence in Chapter 12, but many parents discover that the exuberant boy who used to welcome them into his life with open arms becomes intensely private, even exclusive, during adolescence. Your son will always need connection, but now, in addition to connection with you, he needs connection with a group of friends who understand him, accept him, and share his perspective on the world.

The turbulence and confusion of being a teenager leads boys to form close bonds with friends. Underneath the incessant teasing and joking, there is the sense for many boys that a friend is someone who is "always there for me," someone he can trust implicitly. They may be partners in crime (and the occasional party) or partners in study, but the friendship of adolescent boys can run surprisingly deep.

You may feel a bit left out, even hurt, by the intensity of your son's involvement with and loyalty to his friends during his teen years. Chances are good that he will not talk to you as openly; after all, one of the tasks of adolescence is building an identity that is separate from parents. Pushing your son to talk, to open up, to share details of his personal life, or to include you in his activities usually makes matters worse. Patience, reasonable limits, and respect are key ingredients in a successful relationship with your teen son.

Though your son's relationships with friends can be turbulent, it is unwise to intervene. Instead, coach your son in the skills he will need to repair his relationships. Encourage him to take responsibility for his behavior, to understand his friends' emotions, and to look for ways to make a situation better. It's best to offer empathy than unwanted advice.

Sports and Competition

Not all boys love sports or want to play them; there are lots of healthy, happy boys who prefer music, computers, or science. Still, many boys participate in organized sports and competition at some point in their lives; for many boys, sports define the way they see themselves and are a path to belonging and significance. Sports can provide a safe connection between a father and son, a comfortable arena in which to explore pride, disappointment, determination, even defeat. Sports can allow boys to learn about themselves and to form close friendships with others. Or sports can cause a boy to feel humiliation, embarrassment, and shame.

Sports and Emotional Expression

Drop by your neighborhood Little League field some afternoon and watch what happens. Out on the diamond, tough boys become animated and expressive; they give high-fives, hug one another, and even cry. Victory is sweet, but defeat is always possible.

Americans love sports, largely because they are a metaphor for the struggles in life we all share. For boys, sports can provide something they may not find anywhere else in their young lives: a safe place to have feelings. With the right coach and parental support, sports allow boys to work hard, to learn about themselves, to risk failure, and to experience the joy of accomplishing something in the company of others. Many boys never forget the season they went undefeated, their first birdie on the golf course, or that personal best in swimming.

 *Question?*

What if my son wants to quit a sport and try a new one?
Boys may worry when they sign up for something. Decide what you want your son to learn from a sport. Then sit and talk together about following through. Boys need to be able to try new activities, and parents need to recognize that not everything will be a good fit.

Of course, both boys and girls play sports. Not surprisingly, though, they approach competition with different attitudes. In a recent survey of young athletes at a soccer camp, girls reported that they play sports primarily to have fun and to be with friends. Boys, on the other hand, play to have fun and to improve their own skills. Boys are more likely to see sports as a way to get into college or even as a profession. As boys get older, the pressure to win increases. More and more boys report that what really matters is winning, no matter what it takes. And that may be where the joy of sports loses its luster.

It's Only a Game

It's been called the Tiger Woods syndrome. Little boys playing a game suddenly become budding professionals with coaches, trainers, and sports psychologists. Stickball played in a dirt lot morphs into highly competitive regional leagues for sixth-grade all-star teams. And fistfights erupt at soccer games as parents jeer at the referees, the opposing players, and other parents.

Many experts believe that children, most of them boys, are being pressured by parents and coaches at an early age to devote huge amounts of time and energy to a sport in the hope that it will become a ticket to fame and wealth. Sadly, much of the benefit (and most of the fun) of youth sports disappears when adults send the message that the only reason to play is to win and to make money.

If your son is involved in sports, it is wise to examine your own expectations. For the vast majority of boys, sports should be play. It should be *fun*.

Alert!

Be cautious about signing your son up for daily groups and activities. Experts such as Mel Levine, M.D., an eminent pediatrician, warn that overscheduling children deprives them of the opportunity to learn to entertain themselves. If you provide daily sports, play groups, and other activities, your son may be unable to simply play in the backyard.

When encouraging your son to participate in sports, you must first examine your own motives. Perhaps you wanted to excel at a sport but were not allowed to play. Or your own sports career was ended by an injury and now you dream of the day that your son can do what you could not. It is wonderful when parents can share a boy's dream, support him in his efforts, and provide encouragement. It is harmful when parents push too hard. Your son should play because *he* wants to; it's as simple as that.

You should also be sure to pay attention at practice and games. Most coaches are involved in sports because they care about young people and want to help them. Some, however, believe that shaming and humiliating boys is acceptable if it leads to victory. While some teasing is part of the process, never allow your son to be mistreated physically or verbally by coaches or teammates.

Even if you cannot closely observe how the coach or other players treat your son, there are other ways for you to tell if the sport is a good fit for your child. You may find your boy waiting by the car with all his equipment half an hour before each practice. Or he may develop a stomachache and refuse to talk before and after practices. Be patient and take time to listen. He may have good reason for his feelings.

One thing you must always keep in mind when your son is engaging in a sport: Remember that your son's worth does not depend on his accomplishments. No matter how hard they work and practice, most boys will never be Tiger Woods or Babe Ruth. Notice your son's effort and improvement; be gentle with his faults and failures. Constant criticism of his play will not make him love sports—or you. Your son can learn a great deal about life, trust, and cooperation from sports. He'll learn best if you help him remember that it truly is only a game.

Bullying and Aggression

Each day, as many as 160,000 children stay home from school. They aren't sick, although they may claim to be. They are afraid. For many children, the walk to school, recess, lunchtime, and even school hallways are fraught with danger. Somewhere, behind a tree or lounging insolently against the playground fence, the bully is lurking.

Bullying is a problem of global proportions, and intervention programs exist in almost every country to deal with children who hurt other children. Still, almost every child can tell stories about watching a bully at work, being bullied himself, or participating in some way in bullying another child. Why this epidemic of violence and aggression?

What Bullying Looks Like

Both boys and girls bully other children, although they tend to do so in different ways. A 2004 KidsHealth poll of 1,200 nine- to thirteen-year-old boys and girls found that 86 percent had seen a child being bullied, 48 percent had been bullied themselves, and 42 percent had bullied another child at some point in their lives. Bullying is about power. The days when the local tough kid grabbed some milk money and gave its former owner a black eye are largely past, although physical bullying still occurs. Bullying these days is often more subtle.

 **Fact**

According to a KidsHealth poll, 53 percent of the boys who have been bullied fight back. Only 38 percent of girls fight back. Boys often fear being labeled a coward if they don't defend themselves. Thirty-two percent of girls tell an adult or ask for help; only 19 percent of boys tell someone or ask for adult intervention.

Bullies usually target children they perceive as unlikely to fight back. A child may become the target of a bully because of his appearance, economic level, ethnicity, or speech. Bullies have become more creative in the way they inflict pain and shame on their victims: They may use insults, racial slurs, or other verbal taunts to humiliate a child. They may use emotional or relational bullying, such as excluding their target from lunch or play. They may punch, throw rocks, or pull hair. Or they may use technology; some bullies use e-mail, cell phones, the Internet, and digital photography to spread insulting messages and pictures to large numbers of peers, virtually overnight.

Why Boys Become Bullies

A surprising number of boys have themselves participated in bullying—a fact many of their parents would be dismayed to learn. Boys in general have a tendency to be more physically active, even aggressive. They may not have solid emotional skills or parents who listen and take time to connect.

Many bullies have been bullied themselves, sometimes by their own parents. Ridicule, overly harsh teasing, or neglect may spur a boy to take his own pain out on those around him. A bully may hurt others because he feels insecure or has suffered a trauma he finds impossible to talk about.

Still, there is no excuse for deliberately causing pain. Parents can prevent bullying by making time for connection, by showing boys how to manage anger and use words to express emotions, and by setting clear limits about hurting others. Schools can help by having class meetings to discuss bullying, shaming, and teasing. Research shows that schools with active, involved principals and trained teachers who are paying attention experience less bullying.

Is Your Son a Target?

Many boys suffer at the hands of a bully at least once or twice during their school years. Here are warning signals that your son may be the target of a bully:

- **Feigning illness.** A child who is being bullied often develops stomachaches or headaches each morning before school or comes home "sick" before recess or lunch.
- **Avoiding school.** A boy who used to love school may begin crying, begging to stay home, or even inventing school holidays.

- **Changing habits.** You may notice that your son has night-mares or can't fall asleep. He may eat less or spend hours alone in his room. He may refuse to go outside to play or begin walking blocks out of his way to and from school or the bus stop.
- **Losing focus.** Your son may have trouble paying attention at school, remembering assignments, or doing his homework. He may seem distracted and spacey.

If your son is being picked on a by a bully, he needs your uncon-ditional support and love. Being bullied often causes a boy to lose a great deal of self-respect and confidence. Create opportunities to listen; let him know about the changes you have observed in his atti-tude and behavior. You can ask gentle "what" and "how" questions to learn more about his day. For example, you might ask, "What hap-pened on the way to school today?" or "You seem quiet and sad; what can I do to help?" You can also ask your son's teacher to pay extra attention to recess, lunchtime, and hallway behavior and to let you know what she notices.

Alert!

Be sure that you do not unintentionally encourage bullying behavior by presenting your son role models who glorify aggression. A bully is not strong or manly. Real men do not need to inflict pain on others to feel secure and confident.

It may be tempting to encourage your son to fight back against a bully, but retaliation rarely solves the problem. You may be able to coach your son in keeping his temper, using humor to defuse the situation, acting brave and walking away, or asking a friend to walk with him when the bully is around. Some bullying situations require adult intervention, however. Be sure you work *with* your son to make a plan.

Making Room for Girls

Most little boys begin life with few prejudices about gender. They're happy to play with anyone who wants to do what they do, regardless of gender. As boys grow a little older, however, they begin to be more aware that girls are just, well, different. Their bodies and voices are different; they like different games and toys. They wear pink a lot. By the age of five or six, many boys have become painfully aware that boys are supposed to act like boys—strong, unafraid, and independent. These are the years when a boy's clubhouse is likely to sport a banner declaring, "No girls allowed!"

From Cooties to Kisses

Part of the reason boys avoid girls (at least when their friends are around) during the growing-up years is because they are beginning to be aware of sexuality. Little boys learn about biology and bodies much earlier these days than used to be the case; they are both attracted by and curious about the little girls they know. If they play with girls, they may open themselves to teasing about being in love ("Roy and Alice sitting in a tree, k-i-s-s-i-n-g . . ."), or even about being gay. Many little boys find it easier to avoid girls altogether—even the girls they may have played happily with when they were younger.

By the time a boy reaches the age of ten or eleven, however, his curiosity is beginning to outweigh his suspicion. Boys have feelings, too, remember, and girls often make good friends. By the time early adolescence has rolled around, boys begin to view girls as potential friends, as well as dates.

Girl Friends Versus Girlfriends

In fact, friendships between boys and girls may widen a boy's emotional repertoire and allow him to experience talking freely about his life for the first time. Friendship with girls may be a boy's first encounter with emotional intimacy and trust. Sexual curiosity plays a role, too, and not surprisingly, boys are often reluctant to discuss these complex friendships with parents.

You can help your son form healthy friendships with girls by being neither too pushy ("Oh, your girlfriend is so *cute!* Would you like me to drive you to the movies?") or too discouraging ("You're way too young to be spending time with girls. Where's your football?") Listen well, encourage respect, and focus on the attitudes you want your son to learn. No one can have too many good friends, regardless of their gender.

Supporting Your Son's Friendships

Every parent dreads watching a boy struggle with friendships—and most do at some time during their lives. Your son may tell you, "No one will play with me." Or "Everyone's invited to Sandy's party except me." Parents sometimes have a hard time knowing when to try to help and when to back off.

Question?

A boy had a fight with my seven-year-old son Jon. Now Jon is the only one not invited to his birthday party. Should I call the boy's mother?
It is rarely helpful to intervene in your son's friendships. Instead, focus on understanding your son's feelings and perhaps helping him find solutions to his problem.

Like it or not, you cannot choose your son's friends for him. Nor does rushing to the rescue when he argues with friends or feels lonely teach him the skills he needs to learn. Your son will undoubtedly bring home friends that you do not like from time to time. Forbidding him to see them usually makes them more attractive. Instead, invite your son's friends to your home where you can observe, model good values yourself, and focus on teaching your son about respect, limits, and character.

Friends are a vital and important part of your son's life. You can support him best by offering him opportunities to meet and connect with friends, by allowing him to learn by experience, and by having faith in your boy to build respectful friendships with boys and girls. When your son's friendships hit bumpy spots (and they will), don't rush to intervene or rescue him. Instead, listen, invite him to talk about his feelings and actions, and focus on teaching character and skills.

Your son's friends are not competition for his love and loyalty. By making room for your boy to love his friends and by teaching him how to be a good friend, you ensure that the bond between you will stay healthy and strong.

CHAPTER 12

The Adolescent Boy

Many parents who thoroughly enjoy their son's little-boy years feel a bit anxious about adolescence. Indeed, your son will change dramatically during his teen years, physically, emotionally, and sexually. Teens are more than defiant almost-adults, however; they are also idealistic, thoughtful, and loyal. As boys make their way through adolescence, they are expected to build an independent identity, learn to manage their own lives, and stay out of trouble. Not surprisingly, boys and their parents often find adolescence a bit challenging.

Understanding the Adolescent Brain

When a boy becomes a teenager, parents often believe that he will need less hands-on parenting. Actually, teenagers need active, connected parents but the relationship must change a bit to make room for a teen's growing independence. Excessive control will create power struggles; permissiveness is dangerous. Your son needs kind, firm parenting and reasonable limits more than ever before.

In their book *Positive Discipline for Teenagers*, Jane Nelsen, Ed.D., and Lynn Lott, M.A., observe that human beings are born twice. The first time, our mothers do the labor. The second time, we do the labor ourselves during adolescence. Lott and Dr. Nelsen quip, "The second time is often harder on our mothers and us." Adolescence has long been viewed as a time of intense

turmoil and change; the words "rebellious" and "teenager" often appear in the same sentence. Still, awareness and effective parenting skills will help you keep your connection with your son and allow both of you not only to survive but to enjoy his teen years.

The Teenage Brain: It Really Is Different

Just as technology has allowed us to understand the brains and development of young children, it has opened a window into the often confusing and tumultuous world of teenagers. Parents are often deceived by the mature physical appearance of teens and expect adult thinking and behavior. When teens make mistakes (they will), lose their tempers (they will), or act impulsively (yes, they will do that, too), parents may feel hurt, surprised, and worried. When teens insist on privacy, stop talking about their personal lives, and retreat into their rooms for hours on end, parents may take it personally. If you understand adolescent development, however, you will be better able to stay connected to your son, set reasonable limits, and help him learn self-discipline and life skills.

Research in the past few years has taught us some surprising things about the adolescent brain. Teenagers may look a lot like adults, but their brains are different. And those differences account for many of the characteristics that adults dislike. You may remember that during your son's first few years of life, his brain was actively growing, forming new synapses at an amazing pace. Late in childhood, the brain prunes synapses that are not needed. Your son's genes, as well as the experiences he has had growing up, determine which synapses (and how many) will be pruned. Then, just as adolescence begins, the brain experiences another spurt in growth—including the addition of hormones.

The Prefrontal Cortex: Under Construction

The prefrontal cortex is the part of the brain responsible for what we call executive functions, such skills as impulse control, good judgment, and weighing alternatives—in other words, all the abilities parents wish teenagers had more of. Unfortunately, some researchers speculate that the prefrontal cortex does not fully mature until a person is around twenty-five years old. This helps explain why teens are so likely to be impulsive (accidents are the leading cause of death for teenagers) and so unlikely to consider consequences before acting.

Adolescence may also affect the brain's circadian (sleep) rhythms. You may have noticed that your son "can't" fall asleep before midnight and then "can't" get up in the morning for class. He may not be avoiding school or defying you; many teens complain that they just can't fall asleep early enough and then struggle to wake up in time for class. (Some school districts have experimented with later start times for high school; attendance and performance seem to improve but after-school sports and jobs are affected.)

Alert!

It is tempting to use the growing body of brain research to change policy with regard to such things as school schedules, driver's licenses, and work for teens. Most experts, however, caution against using this information to set public policy until it has been more thoroughly explored and understood.

Another function of the prefrontal cortex is to help control the emotional centers of the brain. This is where the culprits we call hormones enter the story.

Hormones, Emotions, and Anger

Picture Marcus, a fifteen-year-old boy whose parents have brought him to see a therapist to deal with his anger problems. Marcus is sulking; he thinks therapy is lame. At the same time, though, he admits to the therapist that he doesn't always understand what happens to him.

"Sometimes I have a good day at school. My classes go well, and I get to hang with my friends. Maybe the girl I like even talks to me. Then

I get home, and my mom asks me why I didn't take out the trash. And all of a sudden I'm so *angry.* I yell at her and slam my door. Last week I punched a hole in my wall. I don't know why I do that; my mom is actually pretty cool." Marcus shakes his head. "It's confusing sometimes."

Emotions are powerful things. All boys struggle from time to time to express their emotions clearly and effectively; by the teen years, most boys have difficulty showing feelings, asking for help, or even being truly aware of their own emotional state. As if this isn't enough of a challenge, however, the hormones that accompany the physical changes of adolescence complicate matters even more. Emotions, which often prompt impulsive behavior, are flowing freely, while the part of the brain intended to manage them is not yet mature. No wonder teens and their parents feel so irritated with each other!

 **Fact**

Hormones (especially testosterone) appear to affect a teen's ability to read nonverbal signals accurately. Adults use the prefrontal cortex to read emotional cues, but teenagers rely on the limbic system, the system responsible for gut feelings. Teen boys often read emotional cues inaccurately. For instance, when shown pictures of adult faces expressing various emotions, teens interpret most of them as anger.

It is more important than ever to stay connected during your son's teen years, to use your listening skills to draw him out, and to continue to give him words for his often unruly emotions. As much as possible, remain calm—even when your son is not. (Taking a time-out to cool off is a valuable tool for both teens and parents.) Use active listening skills to help your son identify his own emotions; it may be helpful to share your own feelings, as well as experiences you had in your own adolescence. Remember, even though it may feel deeply personal, much of your son's behavior (and anger) is not really about you.

The Task of Adolescence

Adolescence is a critically important part of healthy human development, but it is rarely simple. Teens have to make sense of several conflicting needs. They want to remain connected to parents and family (although they may not want to admit it). They want adult privileges and opportunities. They may feel anxious about their approaching independence. And they want to fit in with friends, to experiment with new behavior, and to learn things for themselves. It can all feel overwhelming.

Physical Changes

It is inescapable; during adolescence, your little boy turns into something completely new. He grows taller, his muscles thicken, and his voice deepens. Hair appears in unexpected places—or doesn't, which is equally as confusing. His genitals grow and develop, and he begins to experience new urges and needs. These changes often make a boy uncomfortable with parents—especially with Mom—and lead to an increased desire for privacy.

 *Alert!*

A 2000 study conducted by the YMCA found that most teens (78 percent) say they turn to their parents in times of need. Boys are actually more likely than girls to ask parents for advice and help. Boys rely on parents' help most when they are around thirteen; they ask parents for help less often after the age of fifteen.

These outward changes happen at the same time as an important internal change: Your son must begin his journey from childhood to adulthood. This transition is called individuation, and it is not always a simple process. Your son must discover his own identity and begin to consider how to live his adult life. He wants to have fun, which may lead him toward risky behavior; his friends have become extremely important in his life. Boys especially may feel pressure to decide on a career path and to be seen as competent and capable. Your son must discover how to separate himself from you, which is why so many formerly compliant children suddenly become allergic to everything their parents believe.

Supporting Your Son in Adolescence

Wise parents can be a tremendous help to boys in navigating the turbulent waters of adolescence. Your relationship with your son will change during these years, but it need not become distant or difficult. Here are some suggestions to consider:

- **Stay connected.** Even if your son claims that he doesn't care if you come to his sports events or school activities, make time to show up. Just knowing you're present in his life can make a huge difference.
- **Remain an active parent.** Your son needs limits and respectful follow-through while he learns how to make good decisions on his own. Educate yourself about his school and his friends. Set reasonable limits and follow through.
- **Recognize that your son's priorities are different than yours.** You may be concerned about curfew, grades, and household chores; your son is more likely to be concerned with the zit on his forehead and the girl who sits next to him in math.
- **Accept that you cannot control your son.** You can guide, teach, support, and encourage your adolescent son; occasionally, you will have to follow through with an agreement. But you cannot control your son's thoughts, feelings, or actions. He must learn to do that himself.
- **Let go when it is appropriate.** Your son needs room to practice adult skills and attitudes. He will certainly make mistakes, but he can learn a great deal from them if you allow him to. Parents who cling too tightly usually find that their son pushes them away.

Through all of this adolescent change, get to know the man your son is becoming. Change can be difficult for parents and for teens, but change is inevitable when you raise a son. He cannot remain your little boy, but he will welcome your presence in his life when it is offered with love and respect.

Setting Appropriate Limits with Your Son

Remember the list of character qualities you made earlier in this book? That list becomes even more important when your son enters adolescence. Suddenly, you realize that you will not have him forever; a few more years and he will be on his own. Every decision you make during these years has implications for the future. You must recognize who you want this young man to become.

Character and Skills

Imagine that you are teaching your son to drive. You may have begun by talking to him while you drive the car, pointing out the steering, braking, and rules of the road he will need to master. Eventually, your son takes the wheel while you sit in the passenger seat. He operates the car; you are there to offer guidance (and the occasional gasp of shock). At long last, the day arrives when your son drives off alone, while you stand in the driveway hoping you have taught him everything he needs to know.

 **Fact**

A 2000 YMCA study found that not having enough time together with parents was the top concern among the 200 teenagers surveyed. Parents were far more concerned about drugs and alcohol. Spending time with their teenagers was the fourth most important priority for parents. Both parents and teens blame parents' work obligations for not having enough time to spend together.

Life with a teenage boy is a great deal like teaching him to drive. You spend his early years teaching him, by word and action, the skills and attitudes he needs. As he grows, you make room for him to try things himself, with your support and supervision. Eventually he leaves home to live his own life, while you watch, hope, and love from a distance. If you try to steer his life *for* him, he may feel he has no choice but to eject you from his car. Wise parents understand that their task is to teach their son, to support him as he learns, and eventually, to let go and allow him to live life on his own.

Fear sometimes causes parents to control, to overprotect, or to rescue their teenage sons. But there is a better way. You can use the everyday issues of life with your son to teach him responsibility, problem-solving skills, and accountability.

Working and Learning Together

Teenagers believe in respect—if they are treated respectfully. Many teens report that they feel disrespected by parents and teachers, which prompts them to be disrespectful in response. Teens are far more likely to cooperate with limits and rules that they have had a voice in creating and that they know in advance. The best way to set limits for teens is to include them in the process.

Picture a boy named Ian. Ian is fifteen years old. He can't drive yet (unless Mom or Dad is in the car), but he is old enough to go out with friends—and old enough to be interested in girls. Melissa, Ian's mother, is curled up with a book one evening when Ian strolls into the den.

"Mom, can I go to the movies Friday night?" Ian asks with a smile.

"I guess so," Melissa replies, setting down her book. "Who's going along?"

Ian drops his gaze and hesitates before answering.

"Well, Bryce and me—and Megan and Sheila," he finishes in a rush.

Melissa smiles. "Who's going to drive, Ian?" she asks. "And where will you be going?"

Now Ian draws a deep breath. "Well, actually, Bryce and I are going to Megan's house—if you'll take us, that is. And then Sheila will meet us there. And we were actually going to rent a video and just hang out."

"Are Megan's parents going to be home? I don't think I've met them," Melissa says. "Can you give me their phone number?"

Ian rolls his eyes. "Come on, Mom, you're the only parent who needs to meet all the other parents. We're not going to have sex or get into trouble or something. We're just going to watch a movie and have some pizza. Don't you trust me?"

Melissa stands up and gazes at her tall son. "Yes, I trust you, Ian. And we still need to talk about how this evening is going to work."

Making a Plan Together

Melissa understands that her son is not likely to confide all the details of his evening to her. She remembers her own high school years and how intoxicating first romances can be. She also loves her son and is willing to risk his annoyance to ensure that no unnecessary risks are taken. So Melissa, Ian, and Don, Ian's dad, sit down around the kitchen table later that night. Melissa gets out a pad of paper and together they make an agreement about Ian's night out. Melissa writes down the terms of their agreement. (Putting an agreement with your son in writing makes misunderstandings later far less likely.)

1. Ian will give his mom Megan's phone number so that she can make contact with Megan's parents. Ian will be allowed to go to Megan's house as long as one parent is at home the entire time.

2. Don will drive Bryce and Ian to Megan's house. Bryce's parents will pick the boys up and drive them home.

3. Ian must be home by 10:30 on Friday night. Ian argues for midnight (with much eye-rolling and sighing) but Melissa and Don remain firm. They do agree, however, that if this evening goes well, they may consider a later curfew next time.

4. Ian cannot leave Megan's house without calling his parents. If he goes anywhere else without letting them know, he will give up the privilege of going out for the next two weeks.

Melissa, Don, and Ian sign the agreement. Now all that remains is following through. If Ian follows the agreement he has made with his parents, he earns their trust and, perhaps, future privileges. If the agreement is broken, Don and Melissa can follow through without yelling or lecturing. When two weeks have passed, they will make a new agreement, and Ian can try again.

 Essential

You will not be able to prevent your son from making mistakes and poor choices, but you can make it possible for him to stay connected, to accept your help, and to learn from his mistakes.

As your son grows older and more mature, he will want more freedom. You can sit down with him *in advance* and respectfully make an agreement about what will happen and when. By allowing him to participate in the process, you teach him the skills of good judgment and planning. By following through with dignity and respect, you teach trust and accountability.

Curfew, Dating, and Driving

The world seems to become a larger, scarier place when your son is a teenager. Most parents remember the moment their sixteen-year-old son grabbed the car keys for the first time, grinned, and walked out the door. Suddenly, you realize that you cannot control your son, protect him, or keep him out of trouble.

It is normal for a parent to worry during adolescence; after all, the risks are so great and your son will be away from you more and more often. Many teens drink, experiment with drugs, and become sexually active. (More about these challenges in Chapter 15.) College looms; will your son's grades be good enough? If not college, what then? And what about the temper outbursts, the long silences, and the disrespect he may show adults?

Teaching Life Lessons

Rather than focusing on controlling your son's choices and behavior (which is impossible anyway), think carefully about what you want your son to think, to feel, and to decide about himself, you, and the world around him. Each time a new issue presents itself, you can use these life lessons as a guide in setting limits and making agreements.

Unfortunately, lectures and commands are usually ineffective with teenagers, who are highly skilled at using words to provoke power struggles. Rather than having yet another debate with your son, consider using actions rather than words. Nonverbal signals, such as looking at your watch or smiling without saying anything, are more effective with teens than long-winded lectures.

Your expectations and values will not be exactly the same as those of other parents. What matters is that you know your son well and have a good understanding of what he needs to learn to become a capable, responsible young adult. Here are some ideas about common issues that will arise with your teen son:

Curfew

There is no right time for your son to be home. Sit down with him when both of you are calm and talk about his plans and your expectations. How old is your son? Is there a legal curfew for adolescents in your community? How well do you know his friends? Cell phones have made it simple for teens to disguise their actual location; like it or not, there is no way you can have absolute control of your son's whereabouts. Instead, let him know your concerns and agree together on a reasonable curfew. You should also decide in advance what will happen if he fails to come home on time. Be sure that you are willing to follow through before finalizing your agreement.

Driving

In most states, teenagers are allowed to have a learner's permit when they are fifteen-and-a-half and can drive with an adult in the car. Some states, however, are considering raising the age at which a teen can get a driver's license. You should know the exact requirements in your own community. It is also wise to agree with your son about which car(s) he can drive, who will pay for insurance, gasoline, maintenance or repairs, and what will happen if he gets a ticket. Will he be allowed to have friends in the car? To drive after dark? Put your agreement in writing and have your son sign it. You will need to refer to it more than once as he masters this important adult skill.

Dating

Most boys begin dating by going out with a group of friends, but at some point, your son is likely to want to spend time with one friend in particular. Again, it is impossible to control your son's preference in partners or his moment-to-moment behavior. Instead, talk with your son respectfully about your own values with regard to love, sex, and relationships. He may not agree with you, but your own beliefs are a good place to begin a discussion about dating. Do your best to keep your connection with your son strong and to remain askable. Don't be surprised (and try not to take it personally) if your son prefers to discuss dating with Dad or another close male figure, rather than with Mom.

Alert!

Power is extremely important to adolescents, who are actively working on the process of individuation. Teens and parents find themselves engaged in power struggles in which parents insist while teens resist. If your son attempts to draw you into a power struggle, withdraw with dignity, follow through on your agreement, or take time to cool off before reacting.

School

While many boys do well in high school and enjoy their studies, many more would rather be doing almost anything else than sitting in class or wrestling with homework. High school can become the arena for huge power struggles between a teen and his parents as decisions about the future loom on the horizon. It is helpful to know your son's school administrators and counselors and to be aware of his progress, but remember that school is your son's responsibility, not yours. Most teens resent parents who are overly intrusive or controlling; some even fail classes or refuse to do homework to show parents that "you can't make me." It usually works best to sit down periodically with your son and talk calmly about his goals and his expectations for the future.

Enjoying Your Son

It is certainly easy to get caught up in the struggles and worries of adolescence. You may look at your almost-adult son and hear a clock ticking insistently in the background. Time is running out, and there is so much for him to learn. Nevertheless, the boy you have always loved still lives within that changing body, despite the occasional defiance and awkward moments.

You may feel anxious as your son experiments with new behavior and spends more time with his friends and less with you. Many adolescent boys require more privacy than ever before and may retreat into silence when unhappy or angry. You and your son may have difficult moments; he may lie, sneak out, or come home drunk. He may skip school or flunk important classes. He may wreck your new car or have a party in your home when you're out of town. Even the most loving and responsible son will make mistakes, and some of them may be pretty impressive.

If you focus only on your son's behavior, the teen years will be unpleasant for both of you. Instead, concentrate on building a solid relationship. Here are some ideas:

- **Show curiosity.** Teens are often passionate about politics, justice, or social issues. Invite your son to share his beliefs; focus on listening rather than debating with him.
- **Be available.** You may be surprised how often your son flops down to talk with you if you're simply there. You may also consider making a regular lunch date or setting aside time to hit golf balls or share a hobby.
- **Appreciate your son's positive qualities.** Even the most troubled teen has strengths; you just may have to look a bit harder to find them. Be sure your son knows what you like about him, as well as what you worry about.

There is much to love about your adolescent boy. Invest time in yourself and your adult relationships so that you can keep your perspective. Then do your best to relax, focus on teaching character and skills, and have fun whenever you can.

CHAPTER 13

The Importance of Character

C haracter is who you are, not what you do. Many parents believe that if they love their children enough, give them what they want, and carefully control their behavior, their children will turn out to be good people. It doesn't always work out that way. Character—having an innate moral compass and the ability to think and act for oneself—does not come from being pampered or controlled. Nor can it be given to children. Character must be learned.

Teaching Character

In *How to Turn Boys into Men Without a Man Around the House*, Richard Bromfield, Ph.D., says, "Your son's good moral judgment is based on his having a strong character and a great deal of trust in his own values. Children who are raised with discipline alone, but who are not taught and encouraged to act and judge for themselves, may well behave but may fail to morally thrive." Character is far more than mere compliance.

Competence and Capability

As your son grows to manhood, he will face many temptations. Before he can make decisions with confidence, he must have the belief that he is capable; he must know that his decisions matter and that he himself has worth. You may remember that human beings need

a sense of belonging and significance; this basic need is an essential building block of character.

One important way of teaching your son that he is capable and competent is to teach him life skills. Even the simplest tasks of everyday life are opportunities for your son to learn that he can care for himself and for others, that he can make a meaningful contribution to the life of his family, and that he can influence the world around him.

Essential

When you watch a movie or a television program, invite your son to tell you how he would have reacted or what he thinks should have happened. Ask "what" and "how" questions and listen to his answers. Inviting him to think for himself is an important way to teach values.

Teaching life skills may begin when your son is a toddler and you allow him to "help" you push the vacuum cleaner. As gets taller and stronger, you can invite him to place napkins on the table, rinse lettuce for salads, or use a sponge to mop up spills. Notice that these tasks are not dreaded chores. They are opportunities to learn and to share the work of keeping a family running smoothly.

As your son grows, he can learn to cook nutritious meals, do his own laundry, mow the lawn, and change the oil in the car. Your attitude is key: If you approach these tasks as opportunities to teach skills and spend time working together, your son is less likely to be resistant. When the day comes that he leaves home, he will be able to take care of himself with confidence.

Teaching Character by Modeling

From the day your son was born, he has been watching you constantly for clues about how life should be lived. You may as well know from the beginning that the old saying "Do as I say and not as I do" will not work with your son. Like it or not, you are your son's most influential teacher, and your actions teach him his first lessons about character. He will be watching to see how you treat other people, how you behave in public places, and what things you value most.

Children are astonishingly perceptive, especially when it comes to adult hypocrisy. Your actions are a far more powerful teacher than your words; your son will assume that if you do it, so can he. Difficult as it may be, living your beliefs honestly is the best way to teach character.

You may fear that admitting mistakes or appearing less than perfect may damage your relationship with your son. In truth, when you can acknowledge your own errors and admit your failings, your son will be able (with time and practice) to do the same. The only way to teach character is to demonstrate it yourself.

Encouragement Versus Praise

Praise is everywhere. Parents are given sheets of paper with "100 Ways to Praise your Child"; they pay children a dollar for each A on their report cards. Parents applaud every scribbled drawing as the best they've ever seen. Teachers hand out stickers, pencils, and pizza lunches for good behavior; smiley faces adorn acceptable homework papers.

Adults praise children for good reasons: They want to encourage appropriate behavior and they believe praise will build self-esteem. Unfortunately, praise is like junk food; a little bit may be acceptable, but too much can ruin your health.

The Pitfalls of Praise
Praise is usually offered when children succeed at a task or live up to adult expectations. But what happens to the child who tries his best and always falls a little short? And what happens when children begin to need praise in order to feel valued? The boy who shouts, "Mommy, Mommy, look at me!" every time he leaps into the pool may not believe he is acceptable unless Mommy watches and offers praise.

In the aftermath of the tragic shootings at Columbine High School, a number of researchers became curious about what might motivate young men to carry guns into school and shoot their peers and teachers. Did they lack self-esteem? Or did they have too much self-esteem (sometimes called arrogance)? A 1998 American Psychological Association study showed that children who are given constant praise begin to depend on it for their sense of self-worth. These children need to be admired, and when they encounter someone who does not like or admire them, the researchers found, they are more likely to become aggressive as a result.

 **Fact**

Many school self-esteem programs are built on offering praise, even if it is undeserved. A Washington student wrote "fffifit" on an assignment, attempting to spell the word "favorite." The teacher praised him for "the creative expression of a feeling." Teaching him to use the dictionary would have been a better choice. Feedback should always be honest and helpful.

Praise leads children to depend on the opinions of others. A child who is praised too extravagantly and too often may become an approval junkie and begin to need praise from those around him. Too much praise does not build competence, a sense of capability, or character.

The Magic of Encouragement

The word "encouragement" comes from a French word meaning "to give heart to." It is easy to praise children who are behaving well, who earn awards, or who excel at school, but what do you say to your son when he is discouraged, has misbehaved, or is having a difficult day? Praise would be insincere; it is encouragement he needs.

Rudolf Dreikurs, M.D., said, "Children need encouragement like a plant needs water." (In fact, so do all humans, parents included!) You can encourage your son by noticing the small things he does well, instead of waiting until he succeeds at the entire task. For instance, you might say, "You worked really hard at getting dressed this morning. Good for you!" You can offer this encouragement even though his pants are on backward, his shirt doesn't match, and his shoes are on the wrong feet. It is encouraging to say, "Wow! You got four B's on your report card. You must be proud of yourself." It is *not* encouraging to add, "and if you just try harder next time you might make A's."

Alert!

Offering encouragement can be difficult for family members who are used to pointing out problems and failings. Begin a family tradition of looking for the positive. Teach your children to compliment each other, to say thank you, and to notice what is right rather than only what is wrong. Looking for the positive encourages everyone in your family.

Encouragement says, "I see you trying, and I appreciate you." Encouragement allows your son to feel valued and to have a sense of belonging even when he doesn't quite live up to your expectations. Encouragement builds connection—so vital to a boy's emotional health—and helps him learn from his mistakes and gather courage to try again. Encouragement also focuses on the person your son is becoming, rather than the things he can (or cannot) do. Offering loving encouragement is an effective way of nurturing your son's character.

Teaching Responsibility

It is an axiom of parenting that when parents take on too much responsibility, children take on too little. After all, why should your son be responsible when you do everything so well? A little nagging is a small price to pay! Responsibility—the ability to accept ownership of your mistakes and successes, to follow through with a task, and to do what you have promised—is one of the most important elements in good character. It is also one of the qualities that many parents fear their children will never learn.

Responsible Parent, Irresponsible Child

You may help your son with his homework and pick up after him because you love him. But when you are responsible for his everyday needs, what is your boy learning? You undoubtedly want your son to become a responsible young man, one who is reliable, confident, and true to his word. Doing too much for him or failing to teach him accountability, however, is likely to encourage him to be irresponsible instead.

The truth is that the sort of parenting that builds character and responsibility may not feel good to you. It is usually more fun to give your son what he wants (rather than what he needs), and it is undoubtedly more efficient to do household chores yourself rather than making room for your son to try. Your son will learn responsibility when you create opportunities for him to practice. Here are some suggestions:

- **Encourage your son to do whatever he can for himself.** Your son may not do tasks to your standards, but he will learn more by doing them himself than by watching you. If you wait on him hand and foot, he will expect you to continue.
- **Don't punish your son for making mistakes.** Kind, firm parenting and discipline designed to teach will allow your son to admit his mistakes (and learn from them) without fear or shame.
- **Allow your son to experience the results of his own choices.** It is tempting (and may feel more loving) to rescue your son when he gets into trouble, fails to do a task, or is lazy or uncooperative, but it rarely teaches responsibility and character.

- **Follow through with agreements.** Your son will learn trust and accountability when you follow through. Be kind, firm, and respectful and do what you have agreed to do.
- **Teach problem-solving skills.** A calm, friendly discussion is often the best way to help your son understand why things went awry and how he can get a different result next time. Teaching your son how to think is more valuable than teaching him what to think.

Invite Cooperation with Family Meetings

Cooperation is the ability to work with others, to contribute to a shared goal, and to compromise when necessary. Rather than commanding, directing, and expecting, focus on inviting cooperation from your son. He is more likely to cooperate and contribute when you listen to his ideas, invite his suggestions, and work *with* him on making a plan to get things done.

One way of inviting cooperation is to have regular family meetings to offer encouragement and compliments, solve problems together, and enjoy family fun. (You can have successful family meetings when your son is as young as four.) Family meetings should not become gripe sessions. Begin each meeting with compliments for things done well during the week.

You can post an agenda board where anyone can list problems that need attention; then you can brainstorm together for possible solutions. It is usually better to work toward a consensus rather than take a vote. ("Losers" rarely enjoy family meetings.) You can finish your meeting with a snack, a movie, or a family activity. Working together to solve problems teaches children cooperation and allows them to feel a sense of belonging and significance.

Empathy and Compassion

Ask most adults which gender is more likely to feel and express empathy, and most would tell you that girls are more empathic. In truth, boys have a tremendous capacity for empathy, kindness, and compassion; they begin life exquisitely tuned to the feelings of others. Unfortunately, traditional cultural ideas about masculinity and appropriate male behavior sometimes lead boys to believe that demonstrating empathy and kindness is a form of weakness.

The Development of True Empathy

Most parents would agree that empathy, compassion, and sensitivity to the needs of others are important elements in good character. Perhaps more than most such qualities, however, empathy must be nurtured and actively encouraged in growing boys.

 *Question?*

My son is three and is very sensitive. If I cry, he cries. Should I try to toughen him up a little?
The ability to empathize with another's feelings is a gift, not a liability. You can encourage your son's inborn compassion and teach him appropriate ways to express kindness. This world would be a better place if there were less "strength" and more compassion.

In *Parenting from the Inside Out,* Daniel Siegel, M.D., and Mary Hartzell, M.Ed., explore the idea of mindsight. According to Dr. Siegel and Hartzell, "Mindsight is the ability to perceive the internal experience of another person and make sense of that imagined experience, enabling us to offer compassionate responses that reflect our understanding and concern. Putting ourselves in another person's shoes requires that we are aware of our own internal experience as we allow ourselves to imagine another's internal world." Mindsight grows as language skills and abstract thinking develop, but it is also dependent on what a boy experiences as he grows up.

Mindsight allows human beings to connect with each other on an intimate level. It is more than just awareness; true mindsight and empathy lead to compassionate action. Boys are just as capable of heartfelt kindness and compassion as are girls; they are best able to explore this part of their inner world when parents openly encourage these abilities.

Kindling a Kind Spirit

Not long ago, newspapers and magazines featured a story about a young boy who was being treated for cancer. The treatment caused his hair to fall out, and he became completely bald. Rather than allow their friend to suffer embarrassment, all of his male classmates (and several of the girls) shaved their own heads. Wonderful pictures appeared in the news media of smiling children with shining heads, actively demonstrating empathy for their friend.

Boys desperately need the opportunity to learn gentleness and strength, conviction and compassion. The world is quick to teach our boys about toughness but offers few lessons in kindness. Consider making empathy and compassion part of your life together as a family. Here are some ideas:

- **Talk openly with your son about social issues, bigotry, the environment, and war.** Allow him to form his own opinions, but encourage the development of compassion and idealism.
- **Talk about the feelings of others.** When you watch television or the news, or are simply out in your community, you can talk with your son about how people may be feeling and what might be helpful to them.
- **Act on your own ideas.** Demonstrate generosity, kindness, and awareness of others when you are with your son. Actions do speak louder than words.
- **Make caring part of your family life.** You may adopt another family at the holidays, work together for an environmental cause, or march for peace. Be sure empathy is a normal part of daily life in your home.

Remember, as your son enters the world of men, his peers and his culture will teach him what masculinity means. You will have the comfort of knowing that underneath the cool surface your son shows the world beats a kind and compassionate heart.

Spirituality in Your Son's Life

Numerous studies of healthy families have discovered a somewhat surprising fact: Families that appear to thrive, to stay connected, and to launch healthy children share something that can be called a spiritual life. It is important to note that spirituality is not the same thing as religion, nor does spirituality refer to any particular church. True spirituality means having a connection to something that is greater than one person and that provides a source of support during difficult times.

 **Fact**

Recent studies show that eating dinner as a family is one of the most effective ways to prevent emotional and behavioral problems for children as they mature. Turn off the television, gather everyone around the table, and eat dinner together two or three times each week. Talk together about issues and ideas, building stronger connections for all of you.

As they grow, children usually have lots of questions about spiritual issues. They wonder what happens when people die or where babies wait to be born. They may feel anxious about death themselves or angry that good people become ill or are hurt by others. Boys, especially during the teen years, can be intensely idealistic; they talk frequently about what's fair or not fair. Any cause they adopt, whether it is political, social, or cultural, is likely to be pursued with their entire energy.

If a religious institution is part of your family's life, you already have a framework for discussing these issues with your son. Be aware that as your son grows older, he may question the principles or requirements of your faith. (Teens often choose issues important to parents as ways to express their individuation; sons of atheistic parents sometimes become ardently religious!) Your spiritual life and ideas will become the foundation for your son's own inner life.

Simply caring about and connecting with a group, a community, or a cause can be a spiritual outlet, too. Your son's life will be richer (and his character is likely to be stronger) if you encourage him to thoughtfully consider some of the global issues we all face. Listen to your son's ideas (even if you don't agree with his positions) and encourage him to care.

Supporting Resilience and Self-Reliance

You may have noticed that one wave of the self-esteem movement has washed into the world of children's sports. In some leagues, parents have become so concerned about possible damage to a child's sense of self-worth that they no longer keep score. There are no winners or losers; instead, everyone gets a trophy. In some schools, honor rolls have been eliminated because they are "too discouraging" for the children whose names aren't listed. Children are too fragile, apparently, to deal with failure, rejection, or discouragement.

Take a closer look, however, and you'll discover that the kids know exactly who is winning and who the good students are. Perhaps more important, failure, rejection, and discouragement are difficult but unavoidable parts of the human experience. Are we really doing our boys a favor by protecting them?

What Defines Resilience?

Resilience is the ability to cope with discouragement, failure, or setbacks and to be willing to try again. Resilience is an important characteristic of successful people, whether in business, sports, politics, or relationships, and most children are far more resilient than their parents may think. You may know in your heart that protecting your son from hurt and disappointment is not really possible, but you may not realize that this sort of overprotection may actually cripple his ability to be resilient and discourage him from trying anything new.

Essential

Thomas Edison tried more than 100 experiments before inventing a working light bulb. He said later that from each failure he learned something that eventually led to success. You can nurture resilience in your son by not exaggerating his failures (or rescuing him from them). Instead, talk together about what he might be able to learn for the future.

Like it or not, your son is destined to experience frustration, rejection, and even failure. Take time to understand and empathize with your son's feelings, but focus your energies on teaching him to cope with failure and disappointment. What might happen next time? What things can he do or say that will get a different result?

Self-Reliance and Character

Mark Twain once quipped that good judgment comes from experience, and experience comes from bad judgment. Mistakes and successes are opportunities to learn, but surprisingly, many people learn more from their mistakes. If you can teach your son skills and allow him to practice in an atmosphere of acceptance and respect, model empathy and compassion for him, refrain from showering him with empty praise, and allow him to grow his own sense of competence and capability, you may just discover that he becomes a self-reliant, confident person, a man of real character.

CHAPTER 14

Boys and the Outside World

Raising a boy is a complicated process. You must decide on discipline, understand development, and build a connection based on belonging. You must teach social, emotional, and life skills. And you must help your son build character and integrity. Parenting a boy might seem almost simple if this was all it involved, but there's more: There is another world out there. Television, advertising, and popular culture all have a powerful influence on your son, and you may not always know what your boy is learning.

The Power of Mass Media

It is all but impossible to escape culture these days. Technology has seeped into every corner of family life. You probably have a television in your home, and if you're like most American families, you either have a computer or are planning to get one (with Internet access, of course). There are movies, video-game systems, and personal digital recording devices. There are cell phones and digital cameras. And there is advertising. Everywhere you look or listen, there are advertisements designed to sell something. What you may not realize is that a great deal of that advertising is aimed directly at your growing son.

Kids as Consumers

The statistics are staggering. Television is everywhere; there is one television set for every American, and 66 percent of American children have a television in their bedroom (which they watch without adult supervision). Most children watch three-and-a-half hours of television each day; they also spend up to four hours a day at the computer or video-game terminal.

The advertising industry pays close attention to what children are watching. Each year, approximately $15 billion is spent on marketing products to children. In fact, in every prime-time hour of television, there are about sixteen minutes of advertising. When your son settles down with a snack to watch his favorite program, advertisers bombard him with slick commercials designed to sell fast food, athletic shoes, and toys. The effect of television is so pervasive that the American Academy of Pediatrics recommends that children under the age of two watch no television at all.

 **Fact**

Marketing products to children is not a new phenomenon. Decades ago, children bought candy cigarettes that were made of sugar, with colored red tips; children held them between their fingers and pretended to smoke them. Eventually, it was revealed that tobacco companies had promoted them to make smoking more attractive to children.

Advertisers see children as a huge potential market. Children's movies come with commercial tie-ins. Action figures, games, and other branded merchandise are everywhere, and children clamor to have them. Why do advertisers target children? Children not only have money of their own, they exert a strong influence on their parents' purchases. Advertisers know that busy parents often substitute things for time and attention and that parents want their children to be happy. What better way than to give a child the latest, coolest toy?

The Power of Peer Pressure

All children want to feel a sense of belonging and significance. This desire to belong—to fit in—often leads children to mimic their peers. Despite what most people believe, children and teens rarely attempt to make their friends participate in risky behavior or dress a certain way. Peer pressure originates within a child's mind and heart. Because a child wants to belong, he *chooses* to do what the other children do so that he will feel like part of the group.

Advertisers understand the power of peer pressure. They know that if they can persuade enough children that a movie, a toy, or a particular type of clothing is cool, other children will want the same thing. Wise parents are able to say no when necessary; they help their children view television and advertising critically and decide for themselves what is right.

Taming the Television

Not too many years ago, parents and children would gather around the family television set to watch programs together. They watched *Father Knows Best* or *Leave It to Beaver* or, a generation later, *Little House on the Prairie*. Nowadays, though, families rarely watch television together. Ninety-nine percent of American families have a television set; the average family owns 2.75 sets. Family time often means family members are in their own rooms, watching different programs.

Children and teens between the ages of six and seventeen overwhelmingly report that watching television is their favorite after-school activity; they also admit that they watch different programs when their parents aren't around. Numerous studies have linked television viewing to obesity, nagging for commercial products, and aggressive behavior. You must decide what role television should play in your son's life.

Television is not benign entertainment; it has a substantial impact on its viewers, including your growing boy. A 2005 study conducted by Stanford and Johns Hopkins universities found that children who had televisions in their bedrooms scored significantly lower on tests, regardless of time spent on homework. Studies also have shown that children who watch television before bed are more likely to have problems with both bedtime and sleep patterns.

Television may affect a child's ability to learn. Educational researchers such as Jane Healy, Ph.D., believe that television viewing contributes to shortened attention spans and an inability to sit still, listen carefully, and absorb verbal information. After all, even "educational" programs such as *Sesame Street* may train children to expect bright colors, rapidly changing scenes, and high-energy entertainment.

Alert!

The National Institute on Media and the Family reports that since the 1950s, more than 1,000 studies have been done on the effects of violence in television and the movies. The majority of these studies conclude that children who watch television and movie violence are more likely to display aggressive behavior, attitudes, and values.

Television teaches children to be passive recipients of information rather than active, critical thinkers. Contrary to popular opinion, children do not learn language or social skills by watching television. Because much TV humor is based on children who speak and act disrespectfully to parents, real-life children may think this sort of behavior is acceptable.

Perhaps most damaging of all, television occupies hours that would be better spent exercising the imagination, engaging in active play and exploration, and learning about the real world. What can you do to tame the television in your home?

One of the easiest and most obvious ways to restrict the influence of television in your house is to limit your son's viewing time. Yes, the television makes a handy babysitter when you're tired and have work to do. Still, television may do more harm than good. Consider setting a limit on screen time. For instance, you may allow your son two hours each day to spend on television, video games, or computer play. (Homework is a separate issue.) When the time is up, the screen goes off, and your son must find something else to do. You may want to allow television only in common areas. Your son does not need a television in his bedroom, no matter what he claims. It is much easier to monitor viewing time and programming when the television is in a room everyone shares.

Another option for monitoring television viewing is to watch television *with* your son. There is no better way to understand what your son is seeing (and deciding) than by watching with him. Use television programs as a springboard to discussions about issues and ideas; asking questions invites critical thinking rather than passive viewing. Television can be a source of valuable information and entertainment when used thoughtfully.

Lastly, you always have the power to turn off the television! If you watch television constantly, your son will, too. Turn it off from time to time and have a conversation, read a book, or enjoy a shared activity. Television limits real connection and relationship. Be sure you know what your son is seeing—and learning.

Boys, Media, and Violence

Boys who are raised with love, who experience belonging and connection, and who learn to identify and manage their emotions rarely have serious problems with violence as they grow up. But as you have learned, boys in our society are more likely to experience harsh discipline, to struggle in school, and to display intense anger. Sadly, the overwhelming majority of violent crimes committed by juveniles are committed by boys.

Why Boys Turn to Violence

Nowhere is our failure to teach boys emotional awareness more evident than in the disturbing trend of violence among boys and young men. School shootings and assaults make the newspapers, but there are quieter acts of violence that happen every day, from schoolyard bullying to date rape and robbery.

 Essential

Young children appear to be most vulnerable to the effects of media violence because they learn by imitating, cannot distinguish between reality and fantasy, and are more impressionable than older children. It is especially important to restrict the amount of violence your preschool-age son sees.

Most researchers believe that boys who turn to violence do so because they lack the sense of connection and belonging so critical to emotional health. They may be abused or neglected, or they may have experienced something they find impossible to talk about, such as the divorce of parents, harsh criticism, or constant humiliation. Boys who lack connection with parents are more easily influenced by violence in television, movies, and video games—and more likely to see violence as a solution to their problems.

Violence in the media dulls empathy; children who see screen violence are not likely to comprehend the impact real violence has on real people. After all, Vin Diesel keeps going when he's been shot six times; doesn't everyone?

The Power of Connection

Real relationship remains the best way to prevent violence and to keep your boy healthy and strong. Your son needs your time and attention; he needs to know that he matters and has worth, regardless of his occasional misbehavior. As with so many other aspects of raising a boy, time spent listening, talking, laughing, and just being together will keep you close to your boy and allow you to guide him as he faces life's challenges. Teach your son social and emotional skills, encourage empathy and compassion, and stay tuned in to the influence of the world he lives in.

Video and Computer Games

Many parents are happy when their boys turn off the TV and turn on a video game. After all, how much harm can a game do? Boys especially enjoy playing together, cheering one another on as they reach different levels and score points. You might be surprised to learn that 60 to 90 percent of the most popular video games have violent themes. One study found that 59 percent of fourth-grade girls and 73 percent of fourth-grade boys say that their favorite video games are violent. One popular game, *Grand Theft Auto: San Andreas*, already notorious for encouraging players to shoot police officers, was revealed to have secret sexual content that could be displayed with a special code.

There is no question that boys love video games; games appeal to their love of competition and action. Boys with strong and loving connections to their families are unlikely to mimic the aggressive and often illegal behavior featured in many popular games; some even argue that games increase a child's hand-eye coordination and reflexes. But what about boys on the fringes, those without strong bonds to watchful, caring adults?

No study has ever proved a direct cause-and-effect relationship between violent video games and aggressive behavior. Still, there is lots of evidence to suggest a strong connection. A 2005 review of all available research presented to the American Psychological Association revealed some interesting facts:

- **Children who play a violent game for less than ten minutes describe themselves as more aggressive shortly after playing.**

- Eighth and ninth graders who spent more time playing violent video games were rated by their teachers as more hostile than other children and more likely to be involved in arguments with authority figures and other students.
- Boys tend to play violent games for a longer period of time than girls, possibly because many games show girls in subordinate roles.
- Children and teens who are most attracted to violent games are also most likely to be vulnerable to the effects of that violence.

Your boy will almost certainly want to own a game system and play video games; if you don't allow it, he will eventually play at friends' homes. What should you do to manage the effect of video violence on your son? First, pay attention. Video games have ratings and age limits for a reason. Don't allow your son to play games that are too mature for him. Second, watch or play with him. Pay attention to what you see in the games he loves; if they are inappropriate or offensive, kindly but firmly say no and explain why.

Your son needs—and wants—you to be his teacher and guide. You can use the video-game culture to teach lessons about character, compassion, and respect. Decide what you want your son to learn about violence, and then follow through with respect and dignity. The choice is yours.

Keeping Up with Your Kid

Like it or not, your son is growing up in a computer-literate generation. Computers are everywhere; the ability to navigate the Internet and use computers for schoolwork and research has become essential to success in the twenty-first century. Despite its benefits and marvels, however, the Internet also poses risks for young minds. This situation is complicated by the fact that many youngsters know far more about computers and the Internet than their parents do.

The Benefits of Computer Literacy

The same study that found that children who have televisions in their bedrooms score lower on tests found that children who have access to computers score higher. There is no question that computers and the Internet can open a world of information and entertainment to children and teens—with proper parental guidance and involvement.

 **Fact**

> The Internet may be one of the few public arenas where girls and boys are equally adept. Research shows that girls are just as comfortable on the Internet as boys are, but they tend to use it differently. Girls use the Internet for schoolwork, e-mail, and chat rooms. Boys prefer to use the Internet for entertainment and games.

A recent survey by the National School Boards Foundation found that most parents provide computers and Internet access for their children for educational purposes. Children who become comfortable with the Internet may actually watch less television and spend more time reading, playing outdoors, or exploring language and the arts. Parents report that they communicate with their children's teachers by e-mail rather than telephone; e-mail also provides a convenient way for schools and community groups to communicate with families.

What Are the Risks?

The Internet poses real risks for children, too. There are indeed predators who haunt chat rooms in order to connect with vulnerable children. Pornography is easy for children to access, and many sites favored by teens have questionable value. As with all the other aspects of technology and popular culture, you must pay attention to what your son is doing, learn to use filters to monitor his Internet access, and talk openly about the dangers and benefits of Internet use.

Like it or not, the Internet is not going away. It is a powerful tool for learning and connecting with the outside world, and it can provide a way for you to learn with your son. Invest the time necessary to become competent yourself and be sure to set guidelines for your son as he explores this ever-expanding world.

Alert!

Be sure you teach your son never to provide personal information, addresses, credit card numbers, or phone numbers to anyone online. Some sites allow users to search for a street address by entering a telephone number. Your son could unwittingly invite a stranger to your home. Learn to use tracking features so you can monitor the sites your son visits.

Movies, Music, and More

Parents, it seems, never quite appreciate the music their children love. You may heartily dislike rap or hip-hop; your parents probably hated rock 'n' roll, while their parents thought Elvis Presley or Frank Sinatra was dangerous. Generations ago, horrified elders denounced the Vienna waltz because men and women actually danced while holding each other!

You don't have to like the music, movies, and other cultural trappings your son loves to understand and connect with him. Curiosity and a willingness to listen and learn are enough.

Listen and Learn

Imagine a teenager named Ethan, who had mowed lawns and baby-sat his little sister, carefully saving his money for the new live CD by his favorite band. He'd counted his stash twice, then three times, and now he was sure: He had enough!

"Mom!" he called, dashing into the study where his mother sat working at the computer. "You said you'd take me to the mall when I had enough money—can we go now?"

Marilyn, Ethan's mom, laughed at his excitement. "I can't go today, Ethan. I have to finish this project by tomorrow morning. But I'll take you after school tomorrow. Would that work?"

Ethan wrinkled his forehead in disappointment for a moment, and then flashed a brilliant smile at his mother. "Yeah, that's okay, Mom. Thanks!"

 **Question?**

> **My son wants to download music from the Internet, but it's illegal. What should I do?**
> Educate yourself about music downloads and the various sites that offer them. Some charge a small fee while others rely on networks of shared files. Talk with your son about the ethical issues involved and decide together what he should do.

The next afternoon, Marilyn met Ethan outside his middle school, and they headed for the mall. Marilyn followed Ethan into the music store and peered over his shoulder as he grabbed the CD.

"Ethan," she said slowly, "that CD has a parental warning on it. What sort of music is it?"

Ethan rolled his eyes and slumped against the display rack.

"*Everyone* has this CD, Mom. There's nothing wrong with it. You're so overprotective!"

Marilyn paused, thinking. "Well, kiddo, last time I checked you were still just thirteen. But I'll make a deal with you. You can buy the CD if we can listen to it together."

Now it was Ethan's turn to pause. "Mom, well, this CD . . . well, it has the 'f' word in it," Ethan said, looking a bit embarrassed.

Marilyn grinned. "I've heard that word before. I just better not hear you saying it to me. We'll listen to the CD on the way home. Do we have a deal?"

Ethan nodded, looking more than a little uncomfortable, but he dutifully placed the CD in the car stereo as he drove home with his mom. Marilyn didn't pretend to like the music; it was raucous and the language was indeed obnoxious. But she listened calmly to the entire thing. When the CD ended, she and Ethan sat in the driveway for more than an hour, talking about the ideas and issues the music raised.

If Marilyn had simply forbidden her son to buy the music, chances are he would have borrowed it from a friend or hidden it in his school locker. By openly sharing it with her son, she found a way to use it as an opportunity to teach values and to enter her son's world, if only for a little while. Ethan, in turn, learned that his mom cared and that he could trust her with his feelings. When he listened to his music now, he would hear her voice as well as the band's.

 **Fact**

A survey by the YMCA found that parents think they're doing a better job of supervising Internet use than teens do. While 71 percent of parents said they closely monitor their children's Web use, 45 percent of teens say they surf the Web "all the time" or "often" without any parental supervision at all.

Tuning In to Your Son's World

Each generation of parents has struggled to understand the world of its offspring. Culture, technology, and fashions keep changing. Children want to belong, and parents struggle to keep up. It can be difficult to find the balance between setting appropri-ate limits on your son's television, movie, video, and music tastes while still maintaining a warm connection, but it's well worth your time and effort.

Choose your battles carefully. Be curious rather than judgmental when possible, but be willing to set firm, reasonable limits. Always keep in mind the lessons in character that you want your son to learn; they will help you know when to listen and when to act.

CHAPTER 15

Dealing with Risky Behavior

Ask a group of third-grade boys if they will ever drink, smoke, or use drugs, and they will tell you an emphatic no. By the time those same boys are in the tenth grade, however, almost all of them will have tried alcohol; most will have been drunk at least once. Study after study repeats the dire story: Teens—both boys and girls—are using alcohol, marijuana, and other substances regularly. Although it is difficult to understand why this is, there are things you can do to keep your son safe and sober.

Adolescent Immortality

Drugs, cigarettes, and alcohol are not hard to find. Middle schools, high schools, and even elementary schools provide ready access to any youngster who is looking for a thrill. (Yes, even in "nice" communities and "good" neighborhoods.) While some younger children smoke or experiment with drinking, it is in middle school and high school that the real risks appear.

Adolescent Development and Substance Use

Many teens (and many boys) drink for the same reasons their parents do: They feel stressed or anxious (being a teenager isn't always easy), and drinking helps them relax. Alcohol and drugs are also part of a teen's social scene; parties often include booze, pot, and other substances.

According to Dan Kindlon, Ph.D., and Michael Thompson, Ph.D., almost four out of every ten male high school seniors have smoked pot within the past year. Two-thirds of all male high school seniors have been drunk; 7 percent smoke pot every day. Boys are also more likely than girls to try "harder" drugs such as cocaine, heroin, ecstasy, or LSD.

Because teens do not yet have a fully developed prefrontal cortex and are not able to control impulses as well as adults, they are more likely to take risks on the spur of the moment, or because their friends do. They also have a strong need to belong with the group and an inherent desire to show adults that "you can't make me." All of this makes drinking and drug use extremely attractive.

Unfortunately, alcohol does not improve judgment and problem-solving abilities, and the potential for injury or serious trouble goes up when boys drink. Some statistics show that in countries where the legal drinking age is lower, teens find drinking less attractive and do less of it. But in the United States, where alcohol is forbidden until the age of twenty-one, alcohol is a way of having fun and dealing with difficult emotions while demonstrating independence from parents.

The Rites of Male Bonding

Sadly, the ability to "hold your liquor" is often viewed by boys as a rite of passage into manhood. Cool guys drink and party, while nerds and geeks do not. A boy's natural urge to explore and experiment can be misdirected into binge drinking and drug use when friends encourage it, and hangover stories—vomiting, crawling, or passing out—seem funny and admirable. "Man, I was *so* wasted!" or "I can't believe I did that!" are common expressions after a night of partying.

Boys often enjoy the feeling of invincibility that comes from an alcohol-induced high. They want to connect with their friends (and with girls) and find it simpler to do so when they are drinking together. It is often easier for a boy to talk honestly about his fears and feelings when he is drunk—and then to forget about it when he has sobered up.

 **Fact**

According to the August 21, 2005, edition of the CBS news program *60 Minutes*, between 10 and 20 percent of the alcohol sold in the United States is consumed by underage drinkers. Approximately 90 percent of teen drinking is binge drinking—drinking to the point of extreme intoxication or passing out.

Like it or not, most boys will try cigarettes, alcohol, and marijuana at some time during their adolescence. Adolescents believe in their own immortality and rarely worry about the risks inherent in drinking. Experimentation and occasional use does not mean that a boy will develop a real substance abuse problem, but it is reason for parents to be aware and concerned.

Influencing Your Son's Behavior

Many parents fear drug and alcohol abuse more than any other risk factor in their son's early years. And indeed, the dangers are real: teens are killed while driving drunk, they overdose, or they have unprotected sex while under the influence of alcohol or drugs. They may also find themselves in trouble with the police for purchase or possession of an illegal substance, causing heartache and trouble for themselves and their families.

You have already learned that you cannot control your son—much as you might wish to. He must learn to practice good judgment and self-discipline; you can only control yourself. You may worry about drinking and drug use because you experimented when you were younger, and you want to spare your son the problems you experienced. Or you may not like his friends and may worry about their influence on him. No matter how good your intentions, however, attempts to restrict your son's whereabouts, friends, or activities are likely to result in power struggles and conflict.

Pay attention to the aspects of your relationship with your boy that you *can* control. For instance, be aware of how much (and how often) you drink—and why. You are your son's most important role model; if you drink to relax or because you are stressed, you are teaching him that alcohol is an acceptable solution to his problems. If there is a history of alcohol or drug abuse in your family, it can be helpful to share that information with your son and to let him know that he may be at risk. (Some experts believe that genes play an important role in how we metabolize and react to alcohol.)

Alert!

A Columbia University study found that the risk for substance abuse may be higher in affluent communities. Boys feel such pressure from parents to achieve and to be admitted to a good college that they resort to substance use to relieve anxiety. In many affluent neighborhoods, boys who smoke or drink are among the most popular in their peer group.

Be aware of your expectations for your son. Do you ask too much of him? How does he react to criticism, high standards, and parental disappointment? Remember that long silences, withdrawal from you, or unexplained changes in behavior may indicate trouble. Focus on your relationship. How strong is the connection between you? As a wise person once said, it is better to know *who* your son is than to know *where* he is.

Talking to Your Son

Too many parents spend a son's entire youth avoiding the subject of risky behavior. "Why bring it up?" they say. "I don't want to give him ideas. Anyway, he's never been in trouble." Hiding from the problem won't make it go away, however. If your son hasn't tried alcohol or marijuana, he undoubtedly has friends who have—and who will offer it to him.

Know Where You Stand

Knowing how to approach your son about drinking and drug use can be difficult, but it is essential that you do so. Your son may be embarrassed or angry; he may believe you're accusing him of bad behavior. The benefits far outweigh the risks, however.

Start by talking about substance use early. You can talk with your son about drinking, smoking pot and cigarettes, or drugs as soon as he is old enough to know what they are. It is not helpful to alarm or frighten your son; simply let him know how you feel about drugs and alcohol. Be clear and consistent from the beginning. He may not always admit it, but your son cares about what you think.

 **Fact**

A YMCA study found that more than half of all parents report talking to their teens regularly about drugs and alcohol, while only 35 percent of teens say parents discuss drugs with them. Teens may be tuning out their parents. Still, it's better to talk too often than not often enough.

You also need to take time to decide for yourself what you think and where you stand. Is it okay with you if your son smokes marijuana? Can he drink, and if so, how much and how often? If you believe he should not use substances at all, how will you set that limit kindly but firmly? You should be willing to give your son clear reasons for your beliefs.

Get to Know His Outlook

You must devote energy to being aware and informed. Make every effort to know your son's friends and their families—not to spy, but simply to create a caring community for all your children. It is also helpful to maintain open communications with his school and other groups. Much teen partying happens right after school, when parents are at work and houses are empty.

Pay careful attention to your son's behavior, and get to know your son's ideas and opinions. Do you know what your son believes about drinking and drug use? What does he see going on around him? If you remain calm, don't lecture, and make yourself available, you may be surprised at how willing your son is to talk with you about drugs and alcohol.

 Essential

Encourage emotional awareness and expression. If your boy can talk about his feelings, fears, and needs, he may be less tempted to mask them with drugs and alcohol. You can't make your son talk, but you can certainly offer to listen.

Keep in mind that if you suspect that your son has a problem with alcohol or drug addiction, don't hesitate to find professional help for him and for your family. You may be unpopular for the moment, but you may also save your boy's life.

Drinking, Drugs, and Driving

Every year, far too many young people die or are seriously injured in alcohol- and drug-related automobile accidents. While having a beer in the backyard with friends may not be appropriate (it is illegal, after all), the risks are far greater when teens party and then get behind the wheel—or into a car with someone else who has been drinking.

As a parent, you *can* exercise some control over when your son drives. Discussions about his driving privileges may be a perfect opportunity to address the issue of drinking and drug use.

Consider making a written agreement with your son. Before your son begins driving on his own, sit down together and make an agreement. Talk honestly about partying and driving. Be sure your son understands that it is *never* acceptable to drive when he has had a drink or used drugs. You may decide that if he violates the agreement, he gives up his right to drive for an agreed-upon period of time. Put your agreement in writing and sign it together, and then be willing to follow through if necessary.

Be sure to let your son know that if he breaks the law, you will not rescue him. It is illegal for teens to purchase, possess, or consume alcohol; marijuana and other drugs are also illegal. Be sure your son knows that if he chooses to break the law, he will be responsible for the consequences. You can support him without rescuing him.

Talk about what your son should do if he is without a safe ride. Agree with your son that if he drinks or is riding with someone who becomes drunk, he should *always* call you. Tell him that there will be no questions or lectures. His safety is most important—even if he is somewhere he's not supposed to be. (Be sure you can follow through with respect and dignity.) You will need to repeat this discussion throughout your son's adolescence.

You cannot afford *not* to have this discussion; neither can your son. Privately, you may believe that the law is too harsh or that a little partying won't really hurt your son, but keep in mind that the risks to your boy are serious and quite real. Talk openly and often with him about drugs and alcohol, driving, and partying.

What about Your Past?

If you're raising a boy these days, chances are good that you, too, grew up in an era when drugs and alcohol were readily available. Many parents have their own memories of parties, sneaking past parents, and occasionally, some serious problems. You may believe that having a strong, open relationship with your son is important, but what if he expects that relationship to go both ways? You must think about what to do if your boy asks you about your own past behavior.

Even the best parent can fall prey to the fear of looking less-than-perfect in a son's eyes. Boys want to love and respect their parents, and parents want to be admired and respected. It can be difficult to find that you have fallen off your pedestal, but telling your own truth may be a powerful way of reaching out to your son.

Question?

I know my son and his friends plan to drink after the prom, and I'm worried that they'll drive. Should I provide a keg at my house? Providing alcohol to minors is illegal in most communities. Your behavior would also tell your son that drinking is okay. Instead, consider getting together with other parents and hosting an alcohol-free, safe and sober prom party. Provide music and activities that will compensate for the absence of alcohol.

Rather than glamorizing your own past exploits, take time to consider the lessons you want your son to learn. What do you want him to believe and decide about drinking and partying? If he asks (and most boys eventually do), you can share with him your own experiences, what you felt and thought, and most important, what you learned—or failed to learn. Remember, real discipline is teaching; sometimes an honest conversation can be the most effective discipline of all. Being real with your son may actually strengthen your connection.

Spying on Your Son

When you love your son, worry and fear can become constant companions. Novelist Barbara Kingsolver once wrote that being a parent means forever walking around with your heart outside your body. When it's late at night, the house is quiet, and you're not absolutely sure where your son is, you may be tempted to wander into his room and search for clues. But what happens if you find what you're looking for?

The Fragile Bond

Most boys (especially teenagers) consider their rooms to be private spaces. They are fiercely protective of their privacy and can become extremely angry when an anxious parent dares to open drawers or sift through a backpack. Parents sometimes believe that their desire to protect a son gives them the right to read journals and e-mail, rummage through closets, eavesdrop on conversations, and even install hidden cameras, but boys rarely agree.

It takes years of work to build trust between a parent and a child, years of listening, sharing, and solving problems together. It is all too easy to damage that trust, and it is not always children who cause the damage.

Alert!

Finding the marijuana your son has stashed under his socks may keep him from hiding it there again, but it is unlikely to improve either your relationship or his behavior.

Yes, you should be aware of your son's activities. It is entirely possible that there would be fewer school shootings and less juvenile crime if more parents were paying attention. Still, the best answer is to begin in your boy's earliest years to build a relationship of trust and mutual respect. Real connection often makes it possible to simply *ask* a boy what he is up to. Boys are surprisingly willing to tell the truth and even to ask for help with everything from drinking to stolen money when they believe their parents are willing to listen and work with them to solve problems.

If You Suspect Trouble

If you know your son well, you will know when there is reason to worry. Unexplained absences from school, missing possessions or money, irrational behavior, or drastic changes in sleep or eating habits can be warning signals. It's usually wise to approach your son directly, calmly, and respectfully and to let him know you're concerned about his safety and welfare—and that you want to help, not bust him.

If your son refuses to talk to you, however, you may decide you have no choice but to search his private possessions. If you find something troubling, talk to your son directly and tell him what you have done and why. Then focus on finding solutions, whatever that may mean. Be sure the message of love and concern gets through to your son.

Without good reason to spy, it's usually better to honor your son's privacy in the same way you expect him to honor yours. If you focus on listening, understanding, and truly connecting, you just may find that snooping is never necessary.

Smoking in the Boys' Room

Compared to the dangers of alcohol, marijuana, and other drugs, cigarettes may seem innocent, even benign. Yet the statistics are staggering; cigarettes, smokeless tobacco, and other trendy products such as clove cigarettes cause nicotine dependence, illness, and serious long-term health risks. Boys begin smoking for a variety of reasons. They may believe it looks cool or macho; after all, many celebrities and athletes smoke or chew.

Smoking may also allow an awkward, gangly teen to feel more mature and manly. Rodeos and auto races are sometimes sponsored by tobacco companies; smoking seems normal and acceptable. And many parents smoke; in fact, boys whose mothers and fathers smoke cigarettes are far more likely to begin smoking themselves than boys with nonsmoking parents.

Drive past any middle or high school, and you'll find the local smokers' corner—the spot away from campus where kids hang out to share cigarettes before or after school. Tobacco is undoubtedly the easiest substance for boys to acquire. About 25 percent of high school students smoke; boys who steal cigarettes from parents or borrow chew from friends or older siblings are usually happy to share.

 **Fact**

According to CNN and the Mayo Clinic, nicotine is as addictive to some people as heroin. It enhances the release of brain chemicals that are associated with pleasure, relaxation, and appetite suppression. Adolescent boys typically show symptoms of nicotine dependence in about 180 days; two-thirds of teen smokers have made at least one unsuccessful attempt to quit.

Smoking is not cool or harmless. Nicotine is highly addictive, and some experts estimate that as many as one out of three smokers will die of a tobacco-related illness. People who begin smoking before the age of sixteen are more likely to become lifelong smokers. There also appears to be a link between smoking, academic problems, and the eventual use of alcohol and other drugs.

You cannot keep your son from smoking or chewing if he decides to try; tobacco products are simply too easy to get and to enjoy away from parents' watchful eyes. You can, however, influence your son's decision about smoking. Here's how:

- **Talk to your son about tobacco.** As with so many other issues in raising your son, sharing your own beliefs about the dangers of smoking is important. Make it clear to your son that you do not want him to smoke.

- **Quit smoking yourself.** If you smoke, consider quitting. Your actions will send a more powerful message to your son than words alone.
- **Limit access to tobacco.** If you choose to continue smoking, do not give cigarettes to your son or leave them where he can easily find them. Do not smoke in your house or allow your son to do so.
- **Invite your son to understand how smoking affects him now.** Lectures about cancer, illness, and death have little effect on teens—they're immortal, remember? You can point out the amount of money cigarettes cost (and what he could buy instead), the smell, the coughing, and the effect on girls.

Samuel Johnson once said, "The chains of habit are too weak to be felt until they are too strong to be broken." Your son will inevitably be exposed to smoking, drinking, and alcohol as he makes his way through middle and high school, but you can help him make wise choices. Do your best to set a good example; talk to him often about the risks he faces. Above all, spend time together. When your son knows he belongs and has worth in his family, he is less likely to go looking for it elsewhere.

CHAPTER 16

Boys and Sexuality

W hen your son is a toddler, it's hard to imagine that one day the chubby little boy who climbs up onto your lap for a snuggle will grow into a man. As puberty begins, limbs stretch, muscles thicken, the voice deepens, and new hair appears. Less apparent are the internal changes. Young men begin to experience all the pressures, desires, and anxieties that grown men feel. Girls are no longer playmates but potential sexual partners. You and your son may feel overwhelmed by this transformation.

Gender Identity in Boys

As you have seen, it is hard to define just what makes a boy manly. What makes a boy a boy? What allows him to feel comfortable in his own skin as he grows up? And how can parents help a son mature gracefully into manhood? While these questions are often difficult to answer in concrete terms, there are some aspects of gender identity that, when you are familiar with them, may help you to understand your son.

The X, Y, and ABC's of Boyhood

A fetus becomes a boy when it receives a Y chromosome from its father to match the X its mother donates. But boyness is not quite that simple. There are actually a number of genes that influence how masculine a boy will become. Despite the familiar stereotype, there is a

wide variation in normal boy appearance and behavior.

Boys can be tall or short, lanky or chubby, active or quiet. They can love sports and academics and music. It is important to remember that preferences are just that—things your boy prefers. He may demonstrate a competitive spirit on the soccer field, the debate team, or the woodwind section of the school orchestra. Playing the trumpet is no more manly than playing the flute; excelling at football is no more masculine than success in calculus.

 **Question?**

My son is four years old, and he always wants to play with the little girls and enjoys dressing up. Should we be concerned?
Gentleness, creativity, and imagination are traits that belong to both boys and girls. Your son prefers gentle play at this point in his life, but that is not cause to worry. Give him opportunities to experience all the joys of childhood and respect the choices he makes.

It may be helpful to know that children of both genders experiment with sex roles as they grow up, imitating both parents from time to time. Little boys may wander into the kitchen dressed in Mom's high heels, jingling necklaces, and lipstick, while girls may pound nails and throw baseballs. While gender identity is a complex process, most boys eventually discover that they will always be boys and that someday they will become men. Boys watch other males for clues about how to behave; they make decisions by watching the world around them about what men are supposed to be like.

Adolescence and Emerging Sexuality

Boys often have far more questions about puberty and sexuality than they are willing to express. For many boys, there is a glaring discrepancy between what they have always been taught about girls and women, and what their peers and the culture push them to believe about sex. Your son may respect and admire his mother and love his sisters (well, most of the time), but he also feels increasing pressure to prove his manhood—and having sex seems to be the way to become a real man.

Like it or not, many teens (both boys and girls) become sexually active early in adolescence. Teens tend to adopt the culture of their peers and may have very different attitudes toward sex than their parents. They often have multiple partners, and even girls may see sex as both a rite of passage and an entertaining social activity rather than a lifelong commitment. In the world of today's teens, love and sex do not necessarily go together.

An old saying with an element of truth states that girls use sex to get love and affection, while boys use love and affection to get sex. The pressure to prove himself sexually may lead even the nicest boy to treat girls in a cavalier manner. Teach your son that his desires are normal, but respect and kindness are essential.

Teaching Your Son about Sex

You should know from the beginning that if you don't teach your son about his body, sex, and sexuality, his friends will be more than happy to take your place—and far less likely to know what they're talking about. Sex involves far more than a physical act; it is an expression of emotions and intimacy, character and moral values. Your son will be curious about his body and how it works from his earliest years.

Just the Facts, Son

Sex is everywhere in advertising and popular culture; sex is used to sell everything from beer to automobiles and even prime-time television is loaded with sexual innuendo. Nevertheless, Americans (including parents) can be surprisingly squeamish about sex. It is far easier to educate your son about his body and his sexuality when you are comfortable with your own.

It is best to use accurate terms to describe body parts and functions and to remain calm and relaxed while doing so. Your son needs to know that sex is normal and healthy; identifying body parts clearly and calmly will help. While baby talk is acceptable when he is a toddler, it is best to use terms such as "penis" or "breast" as he gets older.

Alert!

It often surprises parents to learn that as many as one in four boys is sexually molested. Teach your son that he controls who touches his body and how. Only parents or a doctor (with parents present) should be allowed to touch his private parts; he should feel confident about saying no and telling a parent if he feels uncomfortable.

Children are usually old enough to know about sex when they are old enough to begin asking. Offer simple answers to your son's questions without embarrassment. For example, if your son points to a woman's breasts and asks what those are, you can tell him women have breasts to feed babies. You might even show him a picture of himself nursing so he can understand. Remember, your son does not need all the excruciating details about sex just yet. Keep it simple; you can add information as he matures.

Keep It Real: Talking about Sex with Your Teen

You may remember the day your mother or father sat down with you to have "the talk," but those days are long gone. Because sex is so widely present in modern life, it usually works best to begin talking about sexuality with your son early. Puberty begins for most boys as soon as ten or eleven. You may not *see* changes, but they are undoubtedly beginning. Keep in mind also that boys often feel a great deal of pressure to know everything about sex (or at least, more than their female partners).

Curiosity about sex is normal. Most boys acquire a copy of *Playboy* or the *Sports Illustrated* swimsuit issue sometime during early adolescence. Masturbation and nocturnal emissions (sometimes called wet dreams) are also normal as boys mature, but they may hesitate to talk with you about these events. It may ease the process if you begin the conversation yourself. For instance, as your boy enters adolescence, you can let him know about the changes and urges he may experience. (Even moms can have these discussions. Your son may feel a bit embarrassed, but he will be grateful for the information.)

Sex in the Real World

Most schools these days offer detailed sex education programs. Your son will learn something about anatomy, what a condom is, and all about various sexually transmitted diseases. Unfortunately, most teens fail to apply what they learn in class to sex in the real world. Your son cannot have too much information about sexual health and safety, and you are still his best teacher.

Give some serious thought to what you want your son to learn about sex and how best to protect him. Before you even begin talking to your son, make sure that you are available and unshockable. Your attitude toward sex is important. If your son learns that you are willing to talk with him and that you are relaxed and approachable, he is more likely to come to you with his questions. Let your son know that you will always want to help him, even if he has made a mistake.

To prepare for a discussion with your son about sex, it is best that you understand the anatomy of sex. Many boys enter puberty and experience sexual urges without ever having been taught what to expect. Accurate information about anatomy and function will be extremely helpful to your son. (If you just can't bring yourself to talk about it, ask a trusted male relative or check out one of the many excellent books available. Let your son know he can ask you questions later.)

You may have to educate yourself first, but be sure you know the facts about risks involved with sex. Sexually transmitted diseases,

HIV, and pregnancy are all too common on high school campuses. Despite sex education programs, many teens believe "it can't happen to me" and fail to take precautions. If you suspect that your son is sexually active (or is even thinking about it), be sure he has access to condoms. His health and safety come first.

 *Fact*

As teens get older, they become less willing to talk about sex with parents. One study found that more than half of fifteen-year-olds report that they rarely or never talk to their parents about sex, while twelve- and thirteen-year-olds talk with parents about sex more frequently. Begin talking with your son about sex while he is young—and still listening.

You absolutely must talk to your son about pregnancy and birth control. Most boys know very little about female anatomy, and many believe that girls can't get pregnant the first time they have sex. Be sure your son understands that condoms do not provide adequate birth control. If he is not mature enough to discuss birth control with a partner, he is not mature enough to have sex.

Even if you believe your son may disagree with your old-fashioned views, share your beliefs about morals and values with him. If you believe that sex belongs only in marriage, be sure to teach that belief to your son from the very beginning. You should also be willing to talk with your son about oral sex and other sexual activities, which are increasingly common among teens (and often not viewed as "real sex"). Be realistic, however. Even boys with solid values may choose to have sex before marriage, and many are afraid to tell parents when problems arise. Morals and sex education are not mutually exclusive; be sure your son has both.

Alert!

When talking to your son about sex, you must also discuss alcohol and drugs. Many teens have sex when they are drunk or high and are unprepared for the consequences. Be sure your son understands that partying may affect his ability to make good decisions.

Most boys crave sexual experience. They may long for it and be terrified of it at the same time. Boys want to appear sophisticated and manly in front of their friends, but they also want genuine love and connection. It can be a hard balance to find for even the most mature young man. Be sure you stay connected to your son during these complicated years and that he has the information he needs to make wise, safe decisions.

Becoming Sexually Active

Your head may be spinning by now, especially if your son has not yet entered puberty. You might prefer that he not even think about sex until he has graduated from college, but you're unlikely to get your wish. Most boys have experimented with some form of sexual activity, from making out to intercourse, long before they graduate from high school.

From Playmate to Partner

When boys are young, girls are nothing more than playmates. When boys reach the age of five or six, they usually realize that girls are different and begin to prefer their own gender for play and other activities. As puberty approaches, however, things begin to change. Some boys are interested in girls while still in elementary school, while others do not appear to care until quite a bit later. There's no normal age.

Inevitably, though, boys figure out that sexual activity feels good and that girls are part of the process. (Interestingly, many boys have close female friends throughout childhood and adolescence and can easily separate love from friendship.) Parents are often caught unaware when sons begin to show interest in girls in that way.

 Essential

Never minimize your son's feelings about a girlfriend—or a break-up. He may not be an adult, but his feelings are genuine and deserve your respect. If your son talks to you about his girlfriends, encourage him to trust his feelings, to be honest and respectful, and to make decisions he can live with.

It may be helpful to check in with your son from time to time to see where he is in the process. It is also wise to think about when you will feel comfortable with dating, kissing, holding hands, and other girl-related activities, and to talk openly with your son about "making out." While these are highly personal decisions and will depend on your own beliefs and values, you should consider your son's maturity, self-control, and ability to make good decisions. If your son is not ready to deal responsibly with the risks of sexual activity, he is not ready to have sex.

Your Role in Your Son's Sexuality

As your son matures and begins to form new relationships, your role in his life will change. Mothers in particular can struggle with a son's growing independence and desire for privacy. While some boys bring their girlfriends home, others prefer to keep their personal relationships quite private. This does not mean they are doing something forbidden.

It is also best to refrain from pressuring your son about girls. You can (and probably should) be interested and aware, but allow your son space to find his own way. If he is not interested in dating, don't push him. If your son appears a bit too interested, you may need to work together to set reasonable limits. Take time to meet his girl-friends (and their parents) if you can; it simply makes life easier for all of you. Encouraging your son to entertain his friends at home may allow you to feel comfortable with his behavior.

Is My Son Gay?

Many teenagers go through a period of uncertainty about their sexuality. Imagine Marshall, a young man who was seventeen years old when he realized that he wasn't quite "one of the guys." "I was drinking and partying a lot," he said quietly. "I told myself I did it because that's what all the cool guys did, and I was on the varsity baseball team. I needed to fit in. But I had feelings I didn't want to admit. While the other guys were talking about girls and whether or not they'd scored, I found myself thinking about guys. It scared me, and I couldn't talk to anyone. I thought my dad would kill me, and my friends would disappear—so I drank. Everyone partied, so that worked okay for a while.

"Then I got busted at a graduation party for being a minor in pos-session of alcohol, and somehow the truth just sort of came out." Marshall sighs deeply. "It was tough, man. I told my parents that I thought I might be gay. My mom cried, and my dad just sat there without saying anything. It took them a long time to accept it. But they do now, and so do I. I'm still smart and athletic, still 'me' inside. Being gay isn't easy, but I know I can have a good life. I'm lucky—my parents have stuck with me the whole way."

Although society may be more tolerant now than ever before, gays and lesbians still face an uphill battle in feeling accepted and in having the same rights to love, family, and privileges as heterosexu-als do. According to William Pollack, Ph.D., between 5 and 10 per-cent of all men (from all religious, racial, and ethnic backgrounds) will recognize during adolescence or early adulthood that they are homosexual.

Despite the strongly held beliefs of some groups, available research tells us that most boys do not choose to be homosexual any more than they choose to be straight. Sexual preference appears to be the result of a complex process, including the sexual hormones that bathe the fetus's brain.

Fact

Many boys (and girls) experiment with same-sex relationships and bisexuality as they grow up; only time will tell a boy's true sexual orientation. Curiosity about sex, gender, and relationships is a normal part of growing up. You cannot choose your son's sexual preferences. Accept him for who he is and be patient.

Many boys who are homosexual suffer depression, shame, and a sense of isolation from peers. Numerous studies show that gay teens are at an increased risk for substance abuse and depression; nearly one-third of gay teens have attempted suicide. Your acceptance and support of your son is crucial to his health and well-being. If your son is gay, educate yourself, deal honestly with your own feelings, and stay connected.

You may have strong feelings about homosexuality; you may be shocked that your son is gay. You may even blame yourself. However, parenting appears to have very little to do with sexual preference. Studies of identical twins and other research appears to indicate that boys become homosexual because they are simply intended to; dominant mothers, absent fathers, and parenting style are not critical factors.

Not surprisingly, gay boys and teens need a sense of belonging and significance just as much as straight boys do. In fact, they usually have an even stronger need for acceptance and unconditional love from parents. Most parents of a gay son find that before they can wholeheartedly accept their son, they must deal with their own emotions and beliefs about homosexuality.

It is wise to recognize that homosexuality has very little to do with traditional notions of masculinity. Gay teens are just as able to be talented athletes as straight teens. They have a wide variety of interests and abilities. A gay boy must make decisions about himself and the world and develop his own preferences and strengths, just as any other boy must do. He needs your love and support.

If your son is gay, it is helpful to look for resources in your community. There are many support groups for gay teens and their families; such groups can help you and your son feel comfortable and secure. If you or your son suspects that he is gay, it may also be helpful to find a skilled therapist to help you adjust, learn, and support each other.

Affection with Your Growing Son

As your son matures, you will likely find yourself adjusting to new boundaries of personal space and touching. Imagine this scenario: Meg laughed as she sat at lunch with her girlfriends. "I walked into Aaron's room last week to put away some laundry, and he was naked. I knocked on his door, but I guess he didn't hear me over the stereo. I don't know who was more embarrassed, him or me. He's a man now, not my little boy. The sad thing is that I feel a bit weird about hugging or touching him now. Is that normal?"

As Meg would learn from her friends, mothers often have some adjustments to make as their sons reach physical and emotional maturity. More than one mom has encountered her son coming out of the shower and been surprised at how much has changed. Fathers, too, must adjust to a son's approaching manhood, but the adjustment is often a bit easier, since they experienced it themselves.

Both parents, mothers and fathers, must learn to set new physical boundaries with growing sons. Chances are good that as he grows, your son will still love to have his back scratched, and hugs remain a wonderful way of expressing love and affection. Many boys find, however, that they want a bit more personal space than their parents are used to giving them.

Many mothers notice that their sons become rude and unpleasant as they enter adolescence. Boys who are just becoming aware of sexuality may need to distance themselves from too much closeness with Mom. The more comfortable a boy becomes with his own sexuality, the more likely he is to once again demonstrate affection and connection with his mother.

If your son squirms away from hugs, kisses, or other physical contact, don't take it personally. It takes time for a boy to adjust to his own changing body, his new desires and feelings, and other changes in his physical landscape. Many boys find that the close physical relationship they once enjoyed with their mothers now feels uncomfortable. Mom is, after all, a girl.

Give your son time and space to feel comfortable as a young adult. It often works best to let him set physical boundaries and initiate touch, although you can certainly ask, "How about a hug?" As your son grows up, you will learn to transform your relationship into one between adults and equals. With your encouragement and understanding, your son will learn to have healthy and loving relationships of his own.

CHAPTER 17

Coping with Real-Life Responsibilities

R aising a boy is a long-term process; the ultimate goal is to guide him toward a rewarding and productive adulthood. Your son will need the skills and confidence to support himself, to make decisions, and to thrive on his own. Yet researchers tell us that more adults over the age of twenty-five live at home with parents now than ever before in history. You must equip your growing son to find success and happiness as an independent adult.

Encouraging Responsibility in Your Son

It is tempting (and often easier) to do tasks for your son. After all, little boys tend to leave a trail of messes behind them, and busy parents usually find it more expedient to do things themselves. But what happens when you're no longer around to cook the meals, provide the money, and find the missing baseball glove? Unless you plan on inviting your son to live in his bedroom indefinitely, he will need to learn how to handle adult responsibilities.

Begin Early

You may remember that self-esteem—a sense of one's worth and ability—grows out of skills and competency. Your son will not magically learn to fend for himself on the day he graduates from high school; his education in responsibility should begin with his first steps. No, he won't be capable of doing much when he

is tiny, but you can begin to teach him valuable skills in small lessons. The wonderful part of this process is that when he is young, your boy will think helping you is fun!

 **Fact**

Involving your son in household tasks is not mean or demanding. Your attitude is important: If you believe that you are teaching your son valuable skills, he is more likely to believe it, too. You are demonstrating love and commitment when you teach him to do things himself and give him age-appropriate responsibilities.

Working and learning together also provides a way to talk, share, and connect. Here are some possibilities for teaching skills while your son is a child:

- **When he is two or three,** he can undress himself, feed himself, take off shoes and socks, rinse vegetables and lettuce, pick up toys, put napkins and silverware on the table, and put clothes in the hamper.
- **When he is four,** he can brush his teeth, choose his own clothes, dress himself, put on shoes, measure and pour liquids, clean up spills with a sponge, sort laundry, put away folded clothes, and pour dry food for pets.
- **When he is five,** he can comb his hair, pack his lunch, make simple microwave meals, use a knife to slice cheese or fruit, make a peanut butter and jelly sandwich, fold laundry, help grocery shop, and push the vacuum cleaner.
- **When he is from six to ten years old,** he can walk the dog, pull weeds or plant flowers, operate the washer and dryer, make his bed, help prepare meals, and empty or load the dishwasher. Older boys may want to have a paper route, wash cars, or mow the lawn.

Of course, he can learn to do these tasks only if you take time to train him and make room for him to practice. Remember, keep your standards realistic. It's also okay to have fun; making a game of work sometimes takes the sting out of it. It is more important for your son to learn new skills in an atmosphere of encouragement than to do tasks perfectly.

Responsibility in the Older Boy

As your son grows, he should take responsibility for more and more of his life. Keep in mind that your son is still a beginner; he *will* make mistakes and can learn valuable lessons from them if you remain calm and understanding.

A school-age boy can and should be responsible for his own homework (you can help, but he will learn only if he does the work), keeping track of sports equipment or other possessions, and personal care. You can make routine charts together to help him remember what must be done and when. As much as you can, teach skills, offer a reminder or two, and then step back and let your son learn from his choices and experiences. Painful as it may be, many people learn more from a mistake than they do from success.

Chores and Allowance

Of all the issues that ignite family arguments, chores and allowance are high on the list. You probably believe that your son needs to help out with chores; you also may understand that he needs some money of his own, especially as he gets older and more independent. Should you pay him for doing chores? If so, how much? And if not, what should you do about giving him an allowance and expecting cooperation?

Chore Wars

Chores are more than jobs you expect your son to do (moaning and whining all the way). Chores and family work are opportunities for your son to learn that he is a contributing member of the family, that he can help others, and that he has useful abilities and skills. Chores will also help him learn to plan ahead, to follow through, and to organize his time. Of course, chores can also become a power struggle as you try to make your son do his work.

 Essential

Chores may be high on your list of priorities, but it is unlikely that your son shares your opinion. What normal ten-year-old would rather be inside cleaning his room than outside playing with friends? Let your son know that helping with chores is part of being a family, and then work together to make a plan.

When your son is old enough to help regularly with chores, consider having a family meeting to talk about each person's responsibilities. Start simple: It is easier to gain cooperation when neither you nor your son feels overwhelmed. Be sure to talk about *when* each task should be completed. You can create a family chore chart or other system to act as a reminder, but it is best to avoid stickers, money, and rewards. (More about that in a moment.)

You may find that your son is happy to cooperate when he has a voice in deciding on chores and schedules, which is why family meetings work so well. Your boy may hate dusting but be quite willing to vacuum or mow the lawn. Making a plan together (and reviewing it occasionally) will help you avoid needless arguments. Chores are a practical way for your son to learn how capable he really is.

Allowance

Parents want money and usually wish they had more of it, so it shouldn't surprise you to learn that children want money, too. Even young children need to learn how to handle money wisely. Many parents give their children an allowance, but allowances usually have lots of strings attached.

For instance, a boy may have to do all of his chores perfectly by the agreed-upon deadline to get his allowance (leading to heated arguments about whether a task was done "right" or "on time"). Or his grades might have to be acceptable. Perhaps he has to be respectful or practice the piano every day. Parents concoct complicated systems for tying a boy's allowance to his performance on chores, at school, or at home. All too often, these systems collapse under their own weight.

 **Fact**

A study once found that seven out of ten times, people will offer their cooperation when they are asked respectfully. Asking and inviting is almost always more effective than directing and expecting. Ask your son for his help instead of demanding it and see what happens!

Your boy needs to learn that there are some things he must do just because he is part of a family. (It's called making a contribution.) Sometimes, paying children to do chores teaches them to expect a material reward for everything they do; the reward becomes the focus of the task, rather than the skills and attitudes to be learned.

Here is a way of dealing with chores and allowance that teaches cooperation, responsibility, and respect:

- **Offer your son an age-appropriate allowance.** Consider the amount carefully—you want to teach him responsibility, not fund his video-game habit. Give him the allowance each week with no strings attached.
- **Do not allow borrowing against the allowance.** If your son wants more money, help him learn that he can save each week's allowance and will eventually have enough for his purchase.

- **Allow your son to decide what to do with his money.** You can take time to teach him about saving, giving to charity, or spending, but he will learn best from his own experience. (You can help by asking "what" and "how" questions, such as, "What would have happened if you had saved your money instead of spending it?")
- **Make chores a separate issue from allowance.** Your boy has chores because he is part of the family; he receives an allowance because he needs to have money of his own. You can use family meetings to discuss chores and money management.
- **Avoid rescuing your son if he makes poor choices about money.** Instead of handing out money, help him make a plan for solving his problem (such as doing extra tasks like baby-sitting or yard work to pay what he owes). Remember, the skills your son learns are more important than the toy he wants.

You will need to sit down with your son from time to time to make sure your agreements about chores and allowance are working well for both of you. Your son may never love chores, but he can learn important skills by doing them.

The Art of Managing Money

When your little boy has it, money will probably burn a hole in his pocket. There are games to rent, candy and cool clothes to buy, and interesting stuff to collect. Your son may no sooner have a few quarters in his hand than he begs to be driven to the store. Not surprisingly, your son does not yet know how to handle money; many adults these days struggle, too. In fact, credit card debt is now at an all-time high while retirement savings are at an all-time low. Parents sometimes need better money-management skills themselves!

Teaching Opportunities

Managing money and keeping a budget is often learned through trial and error—especially error. Who hasn't suffered a bout of buyer's remorse or credit card anxiety at least once?

Imagine this scenario: Pamela was paying the bills after dinner one evening when her eleven-year-old son Jamal came rushing into the den. "Mom, can we go to the mall tomorrow? I want to get some of those new basketball shoes—the cool ones that my favorite player wears!" Jamal grinned at his mother. "Please, Mom?"

Pamela reached over and gave Jamal a one-armed hug before returning to her checkbook. "I'd like to buy you those fancy shoes, but I just don't have the money this month."

Jamal's face fell. "You always say that. Why can my friends get what they want, and I can't?"

Pamela felt irritation rising, but it was quickly replaced by a wave of compassion. Pamela was a single mother, and Jamal's friends usually *did* get more nice things than he did. She decided to help her son understand why she had to say no.

"Sit down with me for a minute, Jamal. I want to show you something."

 Essential

When your son is old enough, take him with you to the bank and open a savings account in his name. You can give him the savings book to keep in a special place. When your son receives birthday or other special money, he may choose to deposit part of it in his account.

Pamela spent about fifteen minutes guiding Jamal through her monthly expenditures. She didn't lecture: She showed Jamal how much she earned and how much his father sent each month for his expenses. She pointed out the rent, the utility payments, and the groceries.

"When everything is paid for," she said, pointing to the calculator, "this is how much we have left over."

Jamal smiled. "But Mom, my shoes are less than that! We can buy them easy!"

Pamela nodded. "Maybe, but what about your new basketball uniform and team fees?"

Now Jamal sobered. "Oh yeah, I forgot about that."

"And what if one of us gets sick," Pamela continued gently, "or the car breaks down or that old washing machine falls apart again? I need to have some money set aside for emergencies."

Jamal was quiet for a moment. "I didn't know you had so much to pay for, Mom," he said. "I guess I can wear my shoes a little longer."

Now it was Pamela's turn to smile. "Well, we may not be able to get those fancy things you want, but I do have money put aside for your shoes. We'll go to the mall tomorrow and have a look. Okay?" And she gave Jamal a warm hug.

Kind and Firm

Opportunities to teach your son about money abound in daily life. A trip to the grocery store, shopping for school clothes, or talking about college can all be moments to help your son learn to make and keep a budget. Children do not automatically understand where money comes from and how difficult it is to earn. After all, they see parents going to the ATM and walking away with a handful of bills; money must be easy to come by!

One of the best ways to teach your son to handle money wisely is to do so yourself. Talk to him about saving, spending, and debit or credit cards. Help him understand the difference between wants and needs and how to plan for both. While your son should never be asked to make important financial decisions, you can help him understand how money is managed in your family.

Be aware that many credit card companies target high school and college students, offering credit card accounts with low limits to "help your student establish good credit." Young adults often misuse these cards, running up debts they cannot pay. Be wary of credit card offers; teach your son the risks of credit.

Delayed Gratification

We live in a "fast food" culture; most of us prefer to get what we want when we want it. One of the hidden pitfalls of pampering children is that they may grow up expecting to receive the things they want immediately—and be seriously unhappy when these things do not materialize as ordered. It is unlikely that your son's future boss, college professors, drill sergeant, or spouse will be as generous as you are.

 *Question?*

My son is nine. He has a room full of toys, but he doesn't appreciate anything. What should I do?

Many children don't take care of their possessions because they have been given too much and do not appreciate what they have. Let your son know that if he breaks or loses something, he must help replace it. Be kind and firm; focus on teaching responsibility and gratitude.

Before you rush out to buy your son the latest cool toy or clothing brand, think about what he is learning. If there is any chance that in the future he may need to earn money, save, wait a while, or appreciate what he has, let him work a bit now for what he wants.

For example, Pamela could let Jamal know that she has set aside forty dollars for new athletic shoes. If he really wants the more expensive shoes, Jamal can find ways to earn the extra money, perhaps by mowing lawns or washing cars. Jamal will have to wait a while to get his new shoes but chances are good that he will take better care of them—and appreciate them more—once he has them.

Should Your Son Get a Job?

Carl owns three movie theaters in a medium-sized community. He has worked all his life and is proud of the success he has achieved. But Carl has a problem. "I can't find good employees," he says, shaking his head. "These kids expect to be paid just for showing up, and sometimes I can't even get them to do that! They talk all the time, are rude to the customers, and sometimes they take candy and food. One or two work hard, but most of them don't know how and don't want to learn. Makes me wonder what will happen when they have to go out and earn a real living."

Most boys decide about the time they turn sixteen that they want to get a job. New cars, date money, and fashionable clothing beckon, and work can't be that hard—can it? A job is a valuable way for boys to learn responsibility, real-world skills, and money management. A job can also take time away from schoolwork, athletics, and other important activities. When is your son mature enough to handle a job?

 Essential

As your son enters the adult world, teach him the value of ethics. Examples of unethical behavior are everywhere these days: Enron, steroid scandals, and political events may teach your son that honesty, responsibility, and principles don't matter—getting ahead does. Teach your son (and model) the values you want him to carry into his workplace and his adult life.

Most employers will not hire a boy until he is sixteen; many also require a valid driver's license. While some employers will limit a teen's hours to ensure he does well in school, others expect long hours and weekend work in return for minimum wage. Whether or not to get a job is a decision you and your son should make together.

Let your son know what your priorities are. For instance, you might agree that he must maintain a certain grade average in order to continue working.

You should also explore what your son should do with the money he earns. Can he spend all of it? Or should he begin saving some for college or a car of his own? Be sure he makes time for activities he enjoys, for getting adequate sleep, and for spending time with friends and family. Your son may need your help as he learns to balance the demands of his employer, his teachers, and his family.

Work can help a boy learn to show up on time, follow instructions, and do his best. Create regular opportunities to talk together about job skills, what he is learning, and ways to make his job part of a healthy and successful life.

Respect, Courtesy, and Manners

If you spend much time around groups of young people, you may notice that behavior and manners have changed a bit from the time you were young. Language is rougher; while many teens are courteous and kind, others no longer offer automatic respect to their elders. Adults often comment that they would never have dared behave the way their children do, but then, times have changed. Or have they?

The Value of Respect

All relationships that work, whether in a family, at school, or in the workplace, are built on mutual respect. In a perfect world, children learn about respect because they see it modeled for them every day. When parents treat each other, themselves, and their children with respect, children learn to do the same. In reality, however, respect can be a rare commodity. And like other attitudes and character qualities, respect must be conscientiously taught.

Much of the music and entertainment that appeals to children and teens is inherently disrespectful. Sitcom families and cartoon kids speak disrespectfully, and everyone laughs; it's not all that shocking when real children try the same approach. Nevertheless, respect is a quality that is still highly valued. It becomes especially important when your son leaves your home and must get along with other adults in order to build a successful, independent life.

 **Fact**

Ensure that respect is a fundamental part of your family life. Talk about respect often; be sure that your son has the opportunity to see it in action. Your son will learn far more when you can practice dignity and respect as a family.

Manners, Profanity, and Other Dilemmas

Most parents are delighted and proud when their little boy politely says please, thank you, and excuse me. Parents are a bit less delighted when the preschool years pass and children seem to shed their manners along with their diapers. If you believe that manners and common courtesy are important, be sure you continue to model and teach them in your family. Your son will make his own decisions about whether to practice courtesy on his own, but he is far more likely to do so if you show him how.

Profanity is sometimes a challenge for parents of boys, especially during the teen years. Cursing and rough language, like other risky behavior, may be viewed by boys as a trait of masculinity. Boys feel manly and sophisticated when they let loose with a barrage of four-letter words. You might tell your son that you know he may curse with his friends, but that you would prefer not to hear that language—and you don't want him speaking that way to teachers or other adults. This lesson will be much easier to teach, of course, if you refrain from using profanity yourself.

Self-Reliance in Action

Letting go is hard. Not only must parents step aside and make room for a boy to build his own life, they must trust that boy—still young and unskilled—to go out into the world and make good decisions. The risks are very real, and parents often cling too long and too hard in an effort to prevent a beloved son from making mistakes.

Self-reliance, confidence, and independence are qualities that can only be obtained in the real world. Your son will learn to stand on his own two feet only if you allow him to practice. If you begin when he is young, he can learn self-reliance in a safe environment, *before* the risks become too great.

Just in case you were wondering, here's a news flash: Your son, no matter how wonderful, loving, and talented, will not be perfect. And that is okay. All he needs to be is good enough—good enough in his relationships, in his work, and in his ability to solve problems.

Your son will have the courage to tackle new challenges—work, relationships, college, or whatever else lies ahead—when you build a solid relationship, offer encouragement and teaching, and then have faith in his ability to manage his life. Taking time to say, "I have faith in you; I believe you can succeed," can make all the difference in the world to a boy just setting out on his own.

Throughout the years you spend together, there will be moments for you to step in to help and moments when you must step back. As your son enters the real world, you can let him go knowing that he has the ability to learn, to grow, and to succeed.

CHAPTER 18

Single Parents and Stepfamilies

R aising a boy is enough of a challenge without complications. But as John Lennon famously said, "Life is what happens while you're making other plans." Although the numbers vary a bit from year to year, approximately half of all marriages will end in divorce; the rate is higher for second or third marriages. About 59 percent of American children will spend time in a single-parent home, and 40 percent will be part of a stepfamily. Half of these children are boys like yours who are affected by divorce and remarriage.

No More Broken Homes

Not so long ago, divorce was a shameful thing. Having a child outside of marriage was even worse. These days there are many men and women raising children on their own, either by choice or because a partner has died or left them. Many single parents eventually remarry; in fact, one out of every three Americans, adults and children, is part of a stepfamily. The stepfamily is now the most common type of family in the United States.

Divorce and remarriage may be more common (and more widely accepted) these days, but that does not necessarily make it easy to live in a "different" family. Single parents and stepparents must deal with all the usual issues of raising a boy, but they must also learn to cope with the challenges unique to single-parent and stepfamily life.

What Is Normal?

A number of years ago, researchers interviewed people across the country to discover what they considered a "normal" family to be. The answer, not surprisingly, was that a "normal" family consisted of two parents, never divorced or separated, and two children. In this so-called normal family, Mom does not work outside the home.

The researchers then reviewed the statistics to determine how many American families are "normal." Their answer? Approximately 7 percent. Despite what you may believe about the way it ought to be, families these days come in all shapes and sizes. And with love, thoughtful planning, and education, *all* families can be wonderful, healthy places for parents and children to live. While boys will grieve a missing parent or a family that has dissolved, they still can grow up capable, competent, and happy.

Alert!

Single-parent families and stepfamilies are often born out of pain and loss. In fact, the "step" in stepfamily and stepparent is believed to come from the Old English term "steop," meaning bereaved. Life in a single-parent family or a stepfamily is more rewarding when adults can recognize their child's emotions, as well as their own, and offer empathy and encouragement.

Divorce and separation are serious matters, however. You have learned just how vitally important connection and belonging are to a growing boy. Unfortunately, when parents separate, families become *disconnected*. Parents have strong emotions to deal with, as well as serious anxiety about money, living accommodations, visitation, and other details. Boys whose parents are not together and who do not love each other find themselves in a no man's land of worry, wanting to protect and love each parent and having little or no voice in what happens.

Where Is Home?

For some children, there is no other parent. Mom or Dad has died or disappeared; some children never know their other parent. For most children, however, there is another parent out there somewhere. Children have a wired-in need to connect with and to love *both* parents, a situation that presents obstacles to mothers and fathers who no longer get along.

In her excellent book on divorce, separation, and remarriage, *Mom's House, Dad's House: Making Two Homes for Your Child*, Isolina Ricci, Ph.D., says that divorce should be approached as the *reorganization* of a family, not its destruction; the parents' goal should be to create "two homes with no fighting" for children.

The details of this process are beyond the scope of this book, but it is essential that even the most wounded and angry adults learn to put their children's needs and feelings ahead of their own. Yes, you must take care of yourself and do your best to heal, but your son depends on you to make his world a safe and stable place. He cannot do it for himself.

Regardless of what has happened to your relationship with your son's other parent, your home is not "broken" unless you decide that it is. Boys can grow up healthy, happy, and capable with single parents, married parents, or remarried parents.

The Effect of Divorce on Boys

Reams and reams of research exist on the long-term effects of divorce on children, and on boys in particular. Some experts seem to believe that divorce and life in a single-parent home permanently damages children, while others claim that children with divorced or separated parents suffer no negative long-term effects. The truth is undoubtedly somewhere in between.

The Truth about Divorce

In an ideal world, a boy lives with his mother and his father, experiences a sense of belonging and significance, and learns to be capable and competent as he grows up. (Obviously, even boys with married parents do not always experience this ideal situation!) When parents no longer live together, life for a boy becomes more complicated, but it need not be impossible.

 **Fact**

Many people believe that children of divorced parents will never have healthy marriages and relationships themselves. Not true! A University of Michigan study of more than 6,000 adults found that 43 percent of the adult children of divorced parents were happily married—about the same percentage as those who grew up in two-parent homes.

There are indeed risks associated with having divorced or separated parents:

- **Boys are more likely to react to parents' divorce with anger, academic problems, truancy, or aggressive behavior** than girls, who may try to please adults by suppressing feelings.
- **Boys are more likely to suffer from depression when the father leaves the home,** especially when a boy is not able to spend time with him consistently.
- **Boys may also lose connection with a mother** because she must work longer hours to provide for the family and keep a home running.
- **Boys may assume blame** for the break-up of a family.

It is worth noting that many of the negative effects of divorce have to do with economics. Men are far more likely than women to maintain their standard of living after a divorce, while women (who still tend to have custody of children) find that their economic level falls significantly. Moving to neighborhoods and schools that are less safe and stable may account for some of the problems boys have in the aftermath of a divorce. It is critically important that fathers continue to offer emotional and financial support to their sons after divorce.

Encourage Emotional Awareness

Boys often mask their emotions in order to appear manly. Boys may want to protect their parents and may refuse to talk about their own pain, grief, and worry, or they may act out their feelings by misbehaving. One of the best ways to help your son through difficult times is to encourage him to identify his emotions and to talk about them. Let him know that no matter how tired or anxious you may be, you always have time to listen to him.

Your attitude is also an important factor in how your son adjusts to divorce. If you consider yourself a victim or look for someone to blame, your son will mirror your beliefs. If you face your challenges, seek healing and help for yourself, and do your best to move into a new life, your son will learn from you.

Divorce is a loss for everyone in the family. You will grieve; so will your son. But you can also help each other stay connected, look for the positive, and hang on to your optimism and faith. Don't try to fix your son's feelings: You cannot do that, no matter how much you love him. But you can offer understanding, encouragement, and support. A wise person once said that a family is any circle of people who love each other. You can make sure that your son always has a loving, connected family.

Coparenting

For a boy, having two parents in separate homes is just plain complicated. For instance, what should he do when he has homework and the encyclopedia is at Mom's? What happens when he has a baseball game and his equipment bag is at Dad's? What if Mom lets him watch television, but Dad won't—or vice versa? And what if he has to do chores at two separate homes? Now, how fair is that?

Coparenting is difficult for parents, too. After all, if it was easy to get along with your son's other parent, you might still be together. Still, with some thought (and perhaps some outside help), you should be able to manage logistics, money, and shared custody in a way that works for everyone.

What Children Need

Your son needs the freedom to love and communicate with both of his parents. It is never helpful to trash-talk your ex-partner, regardless of what he or she has done. Remember, that person is a part of your son. You can give a simple account of the facts without including harsh personal criticism or accusations. Be sure your son understands that divorce is an adult decision: It is *never* a child's fault, although many children feel responsible.

 Essential

Judges often consult with older children before deciding on custody or visitation plans. If your son is older than thirteen, it is a good idea to talk with him about his needs and wishes. Where does he go to school? Where would he rather live? His ideas may help you make decisions that work better for everyone concerned.

Moving between two homes can be complicated for all sorts of reasons. Children do best (as do adults) when there is respect, structure, and consistency. Many experts suggest creating a parenting plan to outline the details of shared custody, visits, education, and all the other issues parents must face. You may write this document yourselves, although some parents find it easier to work with a mediator or other professional. In *Positive Discipline for Single Parents*, Jane Nelsen, Ed.D., and her coauthors suggest including the following issues in a parenting plan:

- **Visitation schedules:** Where will children be for weekends, midweek visits, summers, holidays, and special events?
- **Custody:** Who has legal and/or physical custody?
- **Responsibility:** Who will make which decisions? Can stepparents participate?
- **Education:** What's your plan for school decisions, expenses, and college?
- **Medical and dental care and insurance:** Who will pay premiums and copayments? Who will carry a child on his or her policy?
- **Other insurance:** Who holds life insurance or auto insurance for teens?
- **Mental health care:** Who decides about counseling? Who has access to information?
- **Child care:** Who selects child care? Be sure to include pick-up and drop-off instructions.
- **Parenting education:** Attending a parenting class can be helpful to both parents. Who will decide when, where, and from whom to take parenting classes? Will you attend together or separately?
- **Religious training:** What about church attendance or Hebrew school?
- **Contact with extended family:** How will you handle visits with grandparents, siblings, and cousins?
- **Moving:** Can either parent move out of town and take the children?
- **Activities:** Who will pay for sports, dance, music, and so on? Who will attend?
- **Transportation:** How will you handle transportation to and from activities and homes?
- **Access to school and other records:** Who has it?
- **Tax consequences:** Who gets the deduction?
- **Schedule changes:** How will you deal with things such as business travel or emergencies?

It is also wise to have a back-up plan for resolving disagreements and unexpected problems. It may be helpful to view coparenting your son as a sort of business relationship; you don't have to like each other to do a good job. Respect, courtesy, and cooperation are essential. You may not like your ex-partner, but your son will be happier and healthier when you can work together to ease transitions, create structure, and share information.

Avoid the Tug of War

Children universally hate being in the middle of warring parents. Some parents treat children like the rope in a tug of war, pulling and yanking in an effort to win. This sort of behavior will only hurt your son.

Do your best to handle adult matters yourself; let your son remain a child. Children should never be asked to resolve money issues or ask a parent for child support. They should never be expected to provide information to one parent on the other parent's behavior. ("Does your dad have a girlfriend? Does she spend the night?") If you have reason to suspect that your son is being mistreated or neglected at his other parent's home, you will have to take action. Otherwise, offer respect and allow your son to build his own relationship with his other parent. Focus on providing your son with one home that is filled with love, laughter, and trust.

Life in a Single-Parent Home

Being a single parent can feel overwhelming. There often isn't enough time or money to go around, and finding a moment to take a shower or run to the grocery store without children in tow can be impossible. But life in a single-parent home can also be rewarding. You decide how your home will run; you set the tone of your relationship with your son.

Being Mom and Dad

Single parents sometimes struggle to balance all the responsibilities they carry. And many worry that a growing boy needs a full-time mother and father. Is one parent really enough?

Jim was in the kitchen preparing his famous spaghetti when five-year-old Derek wandered in with Coco, the family dog, at his heels.

"Hey, Dad, is dinner almost ready?" Derek asked, picking up some cheese from the counter and plopping it into his mouth.

"Pretty soon, Bud," Jim replied. "How are things in the front yard?"

"Well, Alex and his family are going camping this weekend up at the lake. And Robert is going to visit his grandparents and cousins, so he'll be gone, too."

Derek was silent for a moment, drawing designs in some spilled sauce. "Dad?" he asked, "Why is our family different? I mean, my friends all have a mom and a dad in the same house. I just have you, and Coco, and my lizard. Mom lives so far away, and I only get to see her sometimes. Why can't you and Mom just be *together?*"

Jim put down his spoon and went over to Derek. "That's a tough question, Derek. But I can tell you that it isn't because we don't love you. Your mom is a great lady and a good mom. And I try my best to be a good father. But she and I, well, we just didn't get along when we were together. We fought a lot, and that wasn't good for you. Derek, our family may look different from your friends' families, but it's still a real family. We have lots of love, and we're working on our problems." Jim ruffled his son's hair and gave him a hug. "Now, are you and Coco ready for some spaghetti?"

It is unlikely that you can be a good mother *and* father, no matter how hard you try. And in truth, your son does not need you to fill the role of both parents. Coaches, neighbors, friends, aunts, and uncles can all provide support, teaching, and fun (as well as a respite for you from full-time parenting). Don't hesitate to ask for help when you need it. A skilled therapist, a single-parenting class, or a support group may provide ideas and encouragement.

Focus on building a loving and consistent connection with your son; be sure that you stay tuned in and find time to talk and listen on a regular basis. One good enough parent in your home is all your son truly needs.

Alert!

Statistics show that the risk of physical and sexual abuse increases when unrelated adults move into a home with children. Your son does not need a parent figure nearly as much as he needs safety and trust. Only invite a potential partner to move in when you are sure he will treat your son with respect and kindness.

Keeping Your Balance

Part of being a successful single parent is learning to take care of *you*. You can and should make time for activities and relationships you enjoy. You may need to learn some new skills: Single parenting requires that you learn to manage money wisely, organize time efficiently, and provide kind, firm discipline.

Regular family meetings will help you and your son solve problems together. Believe it or not, life in a single-parent home presents children with real opportunities to learn skills, to make a contribution, and to feel genuine belonging. Choose your priorities (and battles) carefully; there simply isn't enough time to deal with every issue every day. Be sure you spend your time and energy on the things that really matter.

Stepfamilies That Work

Most of the adults who experience a divorce eventually remarry; the resulting stepfamilies often create interesting combinations of "yours, mine, and ours." Some children in a stepfamily may go back and forth between parents' homes at varying times while others live there full-time. Chores, rooms, space, time, and affection all can generate challenges (and arguments). It's also true that stepfamilies can be filled with love, joy, and hope.

Divided Loyalties

You may believe that when you remarry, it is just a matter of time before you live happily ever after. Unfortunately, expecting adults and children who do not share blood or history to love each other immediately can create disappointment and conflict.

Remarriage creates some interesting questions about love and loyalty. Most stepparents will hear the dreaded words "you're not my real dad (or mom)" at some point in their lives. Conflict with stepparents seems to be part of our cultural heritage; after all, look at how many myths and fairy tales feature a wicked stepmother or a cruel stepfather! Unraveling loyalties—the bonds between parents and children—can be one of the most difficult tasks in building a healthy stepfamily.

Essential

Single mothers can raise sons to be happy, capable adults, but it helps to pay attention to your own attitudes toward men. Be sure that any anger or resentment you feel toward your son's father does not spill over onto him. Boys are particularly sensitive to their mothers' attitudes toward men in general and their dad in particular.

It is usually wise for a boy's birth parent to take the lead in providing discipline and setting limits. If your son does not yet respect or accept your new partner, he may be less likely to cooperate. Work together to set limits; focus on building connection. Trust and respect often develop with familiarity.

Your son will need time to accept your new partner and to figure out that person's place in his life. You cannot control or dictate your son's feelings, but you can encourage appropriate behavior. Stepparents and other adult partners can become trusted friends, mentors, and confidants, even though they are not birth parents. Be patient, offer understanding, and follow through with kind, firm discipline.

Working with Your New Partner

Loyalty can be a problem not just between families but within them. It is natural for a parent to favor his or her own child and to feel less of a connection with a partner's child, but this situation can cause real hurt to everyone. It may seem tempting or even necessary to protect your son from your new partner; you may believe your parenting skills are superior and try to help your new stepchildren. Unfortunately, if you assume authority too quickly, resentment may follow.

When you understand the importance of belonging and significance and focus on creating real connection among family members, working together to set limits and follow through becomes much easier. Regular family meetings will help everyone focus on finding solutions to problems and will help new family members get to know each other better.

 *Fact*

Experts report that it takes an average of two to seven years for most stepfamilies to settle into comfortable rhythms and routines. Your stepfamily will not feel like your original family, but that's okay. Flexibility and patience are essential in building a stepfamily.

Few adults agree completely about parenting, no matter how much they love one another. You and your new partner will need to decide together how you will approach raising your shared children. A good parenting class or a few sessions with a counselor may be a wise investment, and they may save you unnecessary conflict and stress.

Little Men

Couples usually marry with hope, optimism, and confidence; certainly no one expects to be divorced. Yet marriages end, for all sorts of reasons, and parents and their children must go on to find new ways of living together. The challenges of life in a different sort of family can pressure a boy to grow up too soon. Sometimes, too, a parent may unintentionally force a boy to become a little man.

Single Mothers and Sons

Being the single parent of a child whose gender is different from your own can present unexpected problems. Single dads often struggle to understand the development and moods of daughters (let alone fashion an acceptable hairstyle); single mothers do not always intuitively understand the needs of their sons. Even the simplest things can be a dilemma. For instance, if you're a single mom with a seven-year-old son who is too old to enter the ladies' restroom, do you let him go to the men's room alone?

In *Real Boys*, William Pollack, Ph.D., quotes a study of 648 children, eight years after their parents' divorce. It found that boys living with single mothers were five times more likely to suffer from a major depressive disorder than girls living with single mothers. Boys living with single mothers were also more at risk than boys who had a consistent relationship with an adult male relative or friend.

Alert!

One study at Ohio State University found that single fathers are no better at discipline than single mothers. If you are a single mother raising a son, it is important that you learn solid parenting skills and give some thought to your long-term goals. You can raise a contented son, even without the help of a live-in man.

Many successful, healthy men have been raised by single mothers. Still, boys living with single moms sometimes feel they must assume the responsibilities of their missing fathers. Sometimes, too, mothers expect boys to become the new man of the house.

Establishing Healthy Boundaries

There is nothing wrong with expecting a son to cooperate with the work of keeping a home running smoothly. Expecting a boy to do a man's job, however, sets him up for failure. Your son, no matter how loving and mature, lacks the skills to be your partner, and while you can invite his suggestions, you must make the major decisions. There should never be any doubt about who the parent really is. It is not your son's job to shoulder your emotional burdens or to worry about the family finances—although he may do so without being asked.

You can and should tell your son, no matter how old he is, that you are the parent and it is your job to take care of him. You can also let him know that you do appreciate his help and support. If you experience depression or anxiety, don't hesitate to get help for yourself; never expect your son to take care of you.

You may be best able to truly love and enjoy your boy when the boundaries between you are clear, reasonable, and respectful. Take time to nurture yourself and enjoy your life and set your son free to enjoy being young. Parents and sons alike can thrive in a different family.

CHAPTER 19

Getting Ready to Let Go

Many parents discover, to their own surprise, that the hardest part of raising a boy has little to do with school, girls, or misbehavior. The hardest part of parenting is often letting go. One of the paradoxes of raising a child is that when you do your job as a parent well, your child will leave you. Launching a son toward an independent life is more difficult than many parents expect.

Knowing When It's Time to Step Back

Monica and Emilio stood in their son's bedroom, gazing at the empty walls and worn carpet. Raul, twenty, had moved out two days before, taking his furniture and personal possessions to the apartment he shared with three friends near the college campus. "I can't believe he's gone," Monica said slowly, slipping her arm around her husband's waist. "It seems like just last week we were worrying about potty training. Do you think we did enough? Will he be okay on his own?"

As long as your son lives under your roof, you are present to watch over him, teach him skills, and set limits on his behavior. Once your son moves out on his own, however, there is no watchful parent in the next room to make sure everything goes well. By the time your son leaves home, he will need to know how to manage his life effectively, make good decisions, and take care of himself.

 **Fact**

> Letting go is a process that begins when your son is born. You must let go so that he can learn to feed himself and so he will learn to walk. If you have worked together at letting go throughout his childhood, you and your son will be ready when you allow him to begin life on his own.

Chances are good that your son will not realize how much you have done for him until he needs to do it for himself. Beyond the daily necessities of food, clean clothes, and a comfortable place to live, he will discover the realities of medical and dental expenses, insurance payments, bank statements, and income tax. Your son must manage his education or career. And he must know how to keep himself physically and emotionally healthy. The law says that a boy becomes a legal adult at the age of eighteen; he can sign agreements and take on other adult responsibilities and obligations.

Weaning

Sooner or later, mothers must wean their infants from the breast or bottle. This process isn't always comfortable or easy for the baby—or for the mother. Weaning happens in the animal world, too; when a calf or colt tries to nurse after its mother has decided it's time to wean, she butts her baby away with her head. She knows its survival depends on its ability to take care of itself.

In *Parents Who Love Too Much*, Jane Nelsen, Ed.D., talks about the difficulty human mothers sometimes have weaning their young. "A primary difference between animal mothers and human mothers is that humans sometimes allow their emotions to take precedence over the long-term good of their children. A human mother tries to wean her child. The child cries. The mother can't stand it, so she gives in. This mother has just made a huge mistake in the name of love. She has loved her child 'too much' to let that child suffer for the moment—and has just insured greater suffering (for both of them) later on."

 Essential

Helen Keller once said, "Character cannot be developed in ease and quiet. Only through experiences of trial and suffering can the soul be strengthened, ambition inspired, and success achieved." Sometimes, doing the right thing as a parent does not feel good, but giving your son what he desires and making his life easy may prevent him from achieving independence.

Weaning is essential for your son to have a healthy life, but it will not be painless for either of you. A child cannot learn new skills unless a parent steps back and allows him to try—and occasionally, to make mistakes. He must cry until he learns to fall asleep on his own; he will fall down until he manages to keep his balance and walk. In this way, through give and take, teaching and practicing, you and your son will move together toward his independence.

Life Skills and Independence

You may think you've heard all there is to hear about the importance of life skills, but the concept takes on a new urgency when your son announces that he's ready to move out. It becomes even more urgent the first time he calls you to announce he's run out of money, forgotten to put oil in his car, or clogged the plumbing of his new home.

If your son is joining the military or moving out to live in a college dormitory, some (if not all) of his daily decisions will be made for him. If he plans to live in a house or apartment, either alone or with roommates, he probably will need to have a few new skills under his belt.

Teenagers and young adults may resist direct efforts to teach skills, usually because the lessons sound too much like lectures. You may find it helpful to sit down and make your own list of the skills your son will need once he is no longer living at home. (It's even better to do this when your son is fifteen or sixteen and you have a few years to work on it!) Ask yourself whether your son can handle the following tasks:

- **Read care instructions** in clothing and wash and dry them properly.
- **Iron** a shirt and slacks.
- **Sew** on a button and mend a seam.
- **Compare prices, quantity, and quality** when grocery shopping.
- **Prepare** at least six nutritious meals from scratch.
- **Operate and maintain** common household appliances.
- **Check the oil and tire pressure** on an automobile.
- **Decide what to do in case of illness** or a medical emergency.
- **Locate a doctor** or dentist.
- **Balance a bank statement** or access an online statement to manage his account.
- **Prepare a resume,** fill out a job application, and conduct a successful job interview.
- **Understand a lease** or legal agreement.
- **Pay utility bills, credit cards bills, and rent** in a timely manner.
- **File a claim** for medical or automobile insurance.
- **Keep records for income tax** and file a return on time.

You can teach these skills to your son by inviting him to work with you as you do them. Or you can begin putting together a notebook of suggestions and information that he can refer to once he has moved out. You can include favorite family recipes, the names of doctors and dentists, family addresses and phone numbers, and other information you believe will be helpful.

Some boys move out before their parents think they're ready; others linger at home until their parents yearn for their departure. If your son moves far from the family home, you are unlikely to be involved in the routines of his daily life. If he moves just across town, however, you will have to decide what role you are willing to play in his independence.

Be cautious about doling out money once your son has moved out. Take some time to reflect: If you feel like you're being manipulated, you are. You can be both kind and firm as you allow your son to experience the results of his own budgeting (or lack thereof). Instead of rescuing, you can help him plan for coming expenses.

 ***Fact***

One study found that 64 percent of parents say they talk to their children "frequently" about character and values, but children are hearing it only 41 percent of the time. Sixty-two percent of parents believe that teens share their values, while only 46 percent of teens agree. Be sure you talk to your son about values while you still can.

Take some time to consider whether your home will be open for drop-in meals, laundry service, or television viewing. Whether you welcome unexpected visits from your son or find them a nuisance will depend on his intentions. Always keep in mind the lessons you want your son to learn; be sure your actions encourage him to develop self-reliance, confidence, and respect. Coddling your son and cleaning up his messes may seem loving at the moment, but you will not be teaching him to make it on his own.

From Parent to Mentor

Rosa is thirty-seven years old, but her mother still reminds her to put on a sweater when the temperature drops below 60 degrees.

Cameron just returned from four years' service in the army, but he and his father still argue about the girls he dates. It's been said that you become an adult everywhere but in your old home, and there's some truth in the saying. All too often, parents find it impossible to let grown children handle their own lives, dispensing advice on everything from clothing to romance to careers.

 Essential

> Think about how your own parents treated you (or how you wish they had treated you). Did you want to be lectured? Scolded? Given reams of valuable but unasked-for advice? Chances are that your son doesn't, either. Ask him if he wants your suggestions: If he says yes, fire away. If he says no, respect his wishes.

When your son is young, you are responsible for his physical care and for his health and safety. Sometimes managing the details of a boy's life becomes such a habit that parents fail to let go when they should. One of the best ways to create power struggles with a young adult is to continue running his life for him when he is convinced that he's ready to do it himself.

Letting go of your son does not mean abandoning or ignoring him. You can and should continue to participate in his life, but the way you do so must change. It may help you to think of your new role as that of a mentor or coach, instead of an active parent. You are there to offer support, encouragement, and, occasionally, active intervention. But it is usually wise to wait until you're invited before riding to the rescue.

Here are some phrases mentor parents should keep handy:

- Would you like my help?
- Do you want to hear a suggestion?
- What ideas do you have for solving that problem?

- Do you want to know what I think?
- Let me know if you need me.

Becoming a mentor means being connected and concerned, but not overbearing or controlling. Your son is far more likely to welcome your participation in his life when you encourage his independence and celebrate his success.

When Your Son Returns Home

Young men usually leave home with high hopes. They leave for an education, for a new job, or for a promising new relationship. Sometimes, though, the world is not kind to them. It's hard to earn enough money for rent and expenses, and sometimes relationships with friends, roommates, or partners don't work out as planned. The college your son always dreamed of may be a disappointment; he may even flunk out. Sometimes young adults want to move back home. In fact, some young men move in and out several times before they acquire the confidence and skills they need to live successfully on their own.

 **Fact**

The September 4, 2005, edition of *60 Minutes* reported on the 80 million echo boomers born between 1982 and 1995. According to pediatrician Mel Levine, M.D., this generation has been protected by parents and "heavily programmed" by a rigorous schedule of activities. Their desire to please their sometimes over-involved parents may make them less able to function on their own.

Imagine Paula's situation. "I never thought I'd be saying this, but I wish my son would leave." Paula shakes her head. "My husband and I planned to retire and begin traveling; we thought Will would be out on his own by now. But here he is . . ." Paula sighs and gestures down the hall, where music is booming out of a back bedroom.

"I love Will, but he's twenty-seven years old. He still leaves his room a mess, can't cook a decent meal, and expects us to give him money. He says he's looking for a job, but I sure don't see any evidence. I'm getting tired of taking care of him." Paula's shoulders slump. "We must have done something wrong."

No matter how much you love your son, it can be disappointing (and exhausting) when he becomes a full-time boarder. There are times when it makes sense for a young man to return home for a while; you may be more than happy to offer him refuge while he regroups and figures out what to do next. Keep in mind, however, that your relationship has changed: He is now an adult and you no longer owe him a place to live. Discussing the terms of your new relationship in advance will save everyone some heartache.

You have the right to set limits in your own home. If your adult son moves back in, be sure you reach an understanding about the following issues:

- How long will he be welcome to stay?
- Do you expect him to pay rent or contribute money toward groceries and other expenses?
- Think twice about providing special service. Who will be responsible for laundry, meals, and household chores?
- Can your son entertain overnight guests in his room? Do you expect him to return home by a specific time?
- How will you handle alcohol or drug use?
- Will you give your son money or assume responsibility for his bills?

When agreeing on the rules your son will follow when living at home, you will need to recognize that an adult son operates by different rules than the little boy you once raised. It may be unrealistic to set a curfew; many young adults are just beginning the evening when parents are going to bed.

An honest discussion about house rules will help you agree on a plan that works for everyone. For instance, you may decide to give up the idea of a curfew and, instead, ask your son to be quiet and courteous if he returns to the house in the wee hours of the morning.

Alert!

According to the 2000 census, almost 4 million young adults between the ages of twenty-five and thirty-four are still living with their parents. This may be the result of a changing job market and a challenging economy; it may also be partially due to the fact that young adults lack the skills and confidence they need to become independent.

The Empty Nest

When children are young, home is a busy place. There always seems to be something to do and somewhere to go; you may long for peace and quiet and wonder what it feels like to be bored. Then your children move out. And suddenly home feels completely different. The fledglings have flown, and the nest is empty.

There are some unexpected benefits to having an empty nest. Here are some you may not have thought of:

- **It's quiet.** The phone doesn't ring as often, and there is no more loud music—unless you're playing it yourself.
- **The gas tank in your car stays full much longer.**
- **Food, milk, and soda stay in the refrigerator,** and the grocery bill goes down.
- **You can buy things for yourself** when you go shopping.
- **The computer, telephone, and television are yours** to control.
- **The house stays clean,** and there is far less laundry to do.

- **You can be spontaneous:** You can go out to dinner at the last minute, go dancing, or wander through the house naked.

Sometimes, though, having an empty nest hurts. The quiet can be either soothing or depressing. If you have enjoyed a close relationship with your son, you will undoubtedly miss his company, his laughter, and his stories about his day. You may find that you and your partner have focused your energy so completely on your children that you have little connection with each other.

Couples often find the time following a child's departure from home to be one of the most challenging in their relationship. In fact, the empty-nest period is one of the most common times for couples to separate or divorce, even when they have been married for decades. Be sure to make your relationship with your partner a priority as your son approaches maturity; take time to nurture intimacy and enjoy each other.

"Get a Life"

The parents most likely to struggle with grief and a sense of loss—what is commonly called the empty-nest syndrome—are those who have been overly involved with their children. If raising your son has been the central focus of your life for two or more decades, you may find it difficult to fill the empty hours once he leaves.

Many parents, however, find that the period following their children's departure is both rewarding and enjoyable. Because so many mothers work outside the home today, women are more likely to feel a continued sense of purpose and to have friends and activities.

Some research suggests that fathers may be the ones who have the hardest time when children leave. Helen DeVries, Ph.D., an associate professor of psychology at Wheaton College, studied the effects of an empty nest on men and women. She found that even stay-at-home moms tended to look forward to the day their children left home and had made plans to fill their time. Fathers, on the other hand, often failed to anticipate the emotional impact of having a child leave and were more likely to feel regret over lost opportunities to spend time with their children.

What to Do with an Empty Nest

Raising a boy takes years of energy, care, and patience. When he goes off to experience the world, you have the opportunity to focus all of that energy on other things. You will never stop loving or caring for your son, but you can find ways to make these years of your life enjoyable and rewarding. If you haven't considered what you will do when your son leaves home, here are some suggestions:

- **Explore interests you haven't had time to pursue.** You might want to learn a new type of cooking, plant a garden, or learn to fly an airplane.
- **Return to school or get a graduate degree.** You have years of accumulated wisdom and experience; it may be worthwhile to put them to use.
- **Travel.**
- **Plan activities, trips, and events with your partner.** Invest in your adult relationships.
- **Do volunteer work.**
- **Start a business.** You may turn a lifelong interest in interior decorating into a successful consulting business or cater private parties and other events.
- **Improve your health and fitness.** You can take a yoga class, hike with the Sierra Club, or ride a bicycle.

You can be supportive of your son while you devote time and energy to your own needs. Demonstrating initiative, self-respect, and enthusiasm may encourage your son to do the same.

Keeping the Connection Alive

Wherever your son goes, it will remain important to both of you to stay connected and involved in each other's lives. While he may no longer need your full-time care and supervision (or at least, so you hope), most adult sons continue to value their parents' love, wisdom, and support as they build their own lives and families.

"When our son decided to study Spanish in Costa Rica, I felt excited and worried," said Martin. "After all, he'd be gone for six months, and he's never been away that long before. We wondered how we'd stay in touch with him.

"Actually, though, it turned out to be pretty easy. We managed a phone call every week or so. We agreed on a time to call, and he did his best to be at home. And he went to the Internet cafes near the university campus a couple of times a week. In fact, every once in a while he would download pictures from his digital camera, and we could see what he'd been doing and where he had traveled."

Martin smiled. "We missed him a lot, but it was a wonderful experience for him. He became fluent in Spanish and learned a lot about the real world. He says he missed us, too, and was glad to come home, but I know he wouldn't have traded that experience for anything."

The home you have shared with your son will provide him with roots for the rest of his life; your encouragement as he flies and experiences life gives him wings. No matter where your son goes, you can keep the connection between you strong and vital. If you are not already computer literate, take time to learn how to send and receive e-mail. Digital photography will enable you to share pictures and memories, and cards and letters are always welcome. Time never stands still, but the future can hold wonderful times for you and your son.

CHAPTER 20
Celebrate Your Son

O ne of these days you will look around and realize that you have nothing to do. Oh, the house may need cleaning, there may be some shopping to do, or you may have a good novel that you're just dying to curl up with. Perhaps you have a round of golf or a tennis match scheduled with friends, followed by dinner at a favorite restaurant. And you'll realize that you don't need to worry about who is watching the kids: The kids are taking excellent care of themselves.

A Moment for Reflection

If you are just beginning your journey as a parent with a little boy tumbling energetically around the house, you may find the idea of reading an entire novel or playing golf almost laughable. But believe it or not, eventually that day will come. The passing of time, along with the changes time brings, is inevitable for all of us, and one day your son will not need you to feed him, clothe him, or put him to bed.

When a boy is young, it is all but impossible to know who he will become. He is busy wrestling with language, with operating his sometimes uncooperative arms and legs, and with exploring the world around him. Gradually, though, as you listen and spend time together, the person he truly is begins to emerge.

Who Is Your Son?

Boys rarely turn out to be exactly what their parents expected. Some things about your son will make you smile; some may be disappointing. You may have hoped for a professional athlete, a talented musician, or a successful businessman. You may have wanted a tall, blond boy instead of the chubby redhead you received. You may be longing for grandchildren while your son travels the world, in no hurry whatsoever to settle down. Your son may have made a number of choices that you simply don't understand and don't like.

It is unlikely that your son's personality will change. Neurobiology researchers believe that temperament is largely inborn and does not change much over the course of our life spans. Behavior and attitudes, though, *can* change. Rather than trying to force your son to become someone he is not, focus your energy on helping him learn from mistakes and make wise decisions.

If you reflect back on your own childhood and young adulthood, you will probably discover that you have changed a great deal over the years. Life does that to people: We must adapt and learn from our experiences, and hopefully become wiser, stronger people. You may look at your boy and be filled with love and pride; you may shake your head and wonder if he (and you) will survive. Do remember, however, that your son's story is not fully written. He is a work in progress and will always need your faith, encouragement, and wisdom.

Did I Do Enough?

As the years of hands-on parenting come to a close, you will undoubtedly have moments of regret and worry, as well as wonderful memories of shared times. No parent is perfect; all parents make mistakes and errors in judgment. Most lose control and say or do things they regret from time to time.

Your son will not be perfect, either. He has lessons still to learn, no matter how old he is right now. As your lives continue to weave in and out of each other, you will continue to learn, to grow—and to make mistakes. Chances are, though, that if you work at staying connected, your relationship will provide joy and learning for both of you.

Setting the Stage

Take a moment to reflect on your relationship with your own parents. How often did you talk to them after you left home? Were you glad to hear their voices on the telephone line or did you try to hang up as quickly as possible? When they came for a visit, were you sad or relieved when they left? Or did they never come at all? What sort of relationship do you wish you had with your own parents?

You will always be your son's parent. But the way you conduct your relationship once he has reached maturity must change. You may be convinced you know better than your son what he should do, where he should live, and perhaps, whom he should date or marry. And you may even be right. But just as your boy resisted your efforts to control him when he was three or fifteen, he is unlikely to welcome your unsolicited advice now. If you hang on too tightly or intrude too much, your son is likely to want distance rather than closeness.

 **Fact**

Gifted children and teenagers, while intense about their activities, are just as likely to be mentally healthy and happy as their less-gifted peers—unless they have overly demanding parents who focus only on success and achievement. Children with demanding parents may fear making mistakes; they cannot enjoy their accomplishments because they're constantly worrying about the next challenge.

As your son matures, your role becomes that of an encourager. You can guide and suggest, and if you've built a relationship over the years of connection and respect, your boy will welcome your suggestions (well, at least most of the time) as he travels toward real maturity.

In *I Don't Want to Talk about It,* Terrence Real, L.C.S.W., defines maturity in part as the experience of communion and giving. Says Real, "Service is the appropriate central organizing force of mature manhood. When the critical questions concern what one is going to get, a man is living in a boy's world. Beyond a certain point in a man's life, if he is to remain truly vital, he needs to be actively engaged in devotion to something other than his own success and happiness." Your son must find the purpose and meaning of his own life. Your job will be to stay close, to cheer him on, and to offer support when needed—not to do the work for him.

Have Faith in Your Son

No matter how old your son is—and regardless of whether or not he admits it—your son craves your acceptance and your love. He wants you to be proud of him; he wants to know that he is good enough just as he is, even when you're encouraging him to try something new. One of the greatest gifts you can give your son is your faith in him and in his ability to make a success of his life.

 Essential

As your son grows, you can talk with him about people he admires. Help him understand the importance of character; teach him to look beyond mere words, appearance, and material success to the value of a life well-lived. He will have to decide for himself how to live, but you will know that you have taught him well.

Think for a moment about men you have known and respected. You may think of a family member, a favorite teacher, a political figure, or another dad on the block. Perhaps you admire a musician, actor, or artist. Now think for a moment about the qualities you respect in that person. What has made him successful? What things do you particularly admire?

You may discover that there are many ways of being a good man. Success, too, has many definitions. Not all successful, accomplished, and respected men are alike, and your son needs freedom and support to become the man he is intended to be. This is easy to say, but sometimes difficult to put into practice—especially if your son's goals and values in life differ from your own.

All parents have dreams for their children. Eventually, though, all parents must release those children to live their own lives. You can let your son know that you believe in him, even when you may disagree with his choices. Knowing you have faith in him—that you believe in the person he is becoming—will carry your son through many challenges.

Rituals and Traditions

Think of the following situation when imagining the future with your own son. Snow was falling heavily outside as Diana pulled a steaming turkey out of the oven. From the other room came the noise of laughter and conversation; Diana's parents had come for Thanksgiving dinner, along with two of her students who couldn't afford to travel home for the holiday weekend. Diana's own son, Ron, was away at college studying music, and while Diana missed him terribly, she was happy that he'd been able to pursue his dream of studying the clarinet with a gifted teacher.

Suddenly, as Diana and her mother Rhonda stirred gravy and tossed the salad, the doorbell rang. "Goodness," Rhonda said, "who can that be on Thanksgiving?"

"I don't know," Diana replied, hurrying to the door. She had no sooner unlocked the front door than a brisk wind blew snow—and Ron—into the house.

"Ron!" Diana cried, wrapping her tall son in a hug. "I can't believe it! What on earth are you doing here?"

"Are you kidding?" Ron answered, laughing and hugging his excited grandparents, "I drove all night to get here. My dorm room was way too quiet—I just couldn't miss the holiday with my family." He grinned. "Besides, Mom, no one makes pumpkin pie like you do."

Memories are the only part of the past that we get to keep. And for many families, the warmest memories are woven around family holidays, vacations, and special events. From your boy's first birthday celebration to his graduation from high school, the traditions and rituals you create together keep family connections alive.

 **Fact**

Richard Bromfield, Ph.D., points out that childhood encompasses 6,570 days, four presidencies, 1.8 decades, and nearly 1 million minutes. It sounds like a lot of time, yet parents discover that it passes all too quickly. Take time to enjoy your son and to appreciate the present moment while he is still under your roof.

You may not realize that children often value these special celebrations as much as you do. Even when your adolescent son rolls his eyes and sighs deeply, he may still look forward to choosing his own dinner menu, eating it on the special family birthday plate, and finding the lucky coin hidden in his piece of birthday cake.

Family traditions often are passed on from generation to generation; these rituals become sacred spaces in our otherwise hectic lives. Here are a few ideas to keep in mind about family celebrations:

- **Nurture connection.** Regardless of your faith tradition, ethnic background, or history, make every effort to focus your celebrations and rituals on relationships rather than food, gifts, or other priorities.
- **Check with family members about what they value.** As your children grow and your family changes, your traditions may need to change as well. Check in with family members occasionally to see what they truly enjoy and appreciate.
- **Be flexible.** Your son may miss a holiday or two because of work or education, or he may want to invite a new friend to come home with him. Insisting on doing things the way you

always have may discourage your son from participating.

- **Watch your stress level.** Your entire family is likely to enjoy celebrations more when you are relaxed and content.
- **Invite contributions from family members.** Your son may one day want to host a holiday celebration at his own home, or he may make suggestions about food, rituals, or other activities. Welcoming new ideas will keep your traditions alive and strong.
- **Appreciate the moment.** Be sure you take time to breathe and to feel gratitude for the time you share with family—even if yours doesn't always resemble a Norman Rockwell painting.

As your son grows and matures, special times to celebrate and reconnect will become increasingly important to all of you. Take time to laugh and play; find ways to gather your family together even when distance separates you. The bonds of family love truly can grow stronger with the passage of time.

Staying in Touch

Everyone these days is busy. Parents work; children and teens have dozens of activities. Keeping the lines of communication open can be a challenge even when children are young. The process is even more complicated when they move away from home, but it is no less important.

As your son becomes increasingly independent, you can find many ways to convey love, interest, and encouragement, whether he still lives at home or has gone off on his own. Here are a few suggestions:

- **Become techno-savvy.** Learn to send text messages, e-mail, and other quick notes. Receiving a "hi—I'm thinking of you" message in the midst of a busy day can brighten even a stressful situation.
- **Send a letter or card.** Old-fashioned paper greetings are still wonderful, and they can be pinned up on a bulletin board or tucked away in a drawer for later.

- **Make phone calls easy.** Consider getting a family-plan cell phone to make staying in touch easier (and less expensive). You can even supply your son with a prepaid phone card to encourage his calls.
- **Plan a visit.** Your son may not have the time or the money to travel home often and may appreciate a visit from you. Use your common sense; visits usually are more enjoyable when you can recognize that your son also has commitments and interests of his own.
- **Send a care package.** If your son lives away from home, a box filled with food items, books, photographs, or small mementos may be deeply appreciated.

One of the paradoxes of raising a boy is that you may miss him most just as he's learning to love his freedom. It is tempting to call or visit often, but many young men perceive excess attention as intrusive. Making your son feel guilty for not needing you will not improve your relationship. Celebrate your son's ability to thrive on his own; respect his need for privacy and independence. Remember to practice simple courtesy. Your son is more likely to welcome calls and visits when you are sensitive to his needs.

Staying in touch with your son as he matures can be a balancing act. You must allow him space to stretch his wings while still letting him know that you care. Your inner wisdom and knowledge of your son will help you know when to stay close and when to take a step back and let him experience the world for himself.

Congratulations! You Raised a Son

You have learned about infants, toddlers, school-age boys, and teenagers. You have been inundated with tips, facts, tools, and suggestions. But one important thing has been left unsaid: None of this could have happened without you.

Parenting—the art of raising a child to capable, happy adulthood—is underappreciated by society. After all, plenty of people have kids, and every parent should be able to raise one competently. Shouldn't they? Truthfully, however, changes in society and in twenty-first-century families have made raising a boy to confident, successful maturity far more challenging than it has ever been before.

In fact, many women feel more valued by employers than they do by their families. A job offers the sense that you have accomplished something worthwhile. You receive timely feedback, and you are paid for the work you do. Parenting, on the other hand, does not offer such immediate rewards. You must have faith in yourself and your children, and believe that one day your efforts will be worthwhile.

Give Yourself Credit

Think for a moment about your most difficult moments as a parent. Most parents can acknowledge that there have been times when they struggled to be loving, patient, firm, and kind. There were undoubtedly times when you failed to do what you believed you should. And there have been moments when you did not know what to do next, or when you had to accept that you had made a mistake.

 **Essential**

Be sure that you take time—and teach your son—to feel gratitude for the blessings and gifts you enjoy in your lives. It can be helpful to create a family gratitude journal to record the things you appreciate. You can work together to record the special moments you encounter in even the most difficult circumstances.

It may be helpful to know that being less than perfect simply makes you human. The good news is that perfection is not a requirement for being a good parent. You will never be perfect and neither will your son. Rather than blaming yourself for mistakes, failures, and errors in judgment, take a moment to give yourself credit for being there, for offering love and acceptance, and for doing the best you could in a difficult world to raise a capable, competent young man.

Doing the right thing is always easy when you're reading about it in a book or watching one of the many television experts. But real life is different than books or television. Raising a son is a great deal harder when you must face the daily ups and downs of life with an active, curious boy and somehow make decisions that help him learn character and important life skills. You have undoubtedly done the best you could as you raised your son; no one can do better than their best.

Using Your Judgment to Shape a Son

When all is said and done, you must decide what matters most. Take a moment to review the list of character qualities you created for your son. Has he achieved most of them? If you are like most families, there are many successes and a few failures scattered along the path. You have dreams and fears for your boy and regardless of where he goes and what he accomplishes, you will never stop caring about him.

There are no guarantees in raising a son. He has wonderful strengths and some limitations; so do you. Learn to listen to your heart. The love you feel for your boy, your knowledge of the man he is becoming, and your own inner wisdom will guide you in knowing what to do.

Appendix A
Bibliography

Biederman, Jerry, and Lorin Biederman, eds. *Parent School: Simple Lessons from the Leading Experts on Being a Mom and Dad* (New York: M. Evans and Co., 2002).

Bromfield, Richard, Ph.D., and Cheryl Erwin, M.A. *How to Turn Boys into Men Without a Man Around the House: A Single Mother's Guide* (Rocklin, CA: Prima, 2001).

Chess, Stella, M.D., and Alexander Thomas, M.D. *Know Your Child* (New York: Basic Books, 1987).

Colapinto, John. *As Nature Made Him: The Boy Who Was Raised as a Girl* (New York: HarperCollins, 2000).

Commission on Children at Risk. *Hardwired to Connect: The New Scientific Case for Authoritative Communities* (Institute for American Values, 2003).

Dreikurs, Rudolf, M.D., with Vicki Soltz, R.N. *Children: The Challenge* (New York: Plume Books, 1990).

Frontline. *Inside the Teenage Brain* (PBS Video, Public Broadcasting Service, 2004).

Gilbert, Susan. *A Field Guide to Boys and Girls* (New York: HarperCollins, 2000).

Hallowell, Edward M., M.D., and John J. Ratey, M.D. *Driven to Distraction: Recognizing and Coping with Attention Deficit Disorder from Childhood Through Adulthood* (New York: Touchstone, 1995).

Healy, Jane M., Ph.D. *Endangered Minds: Why Children Don't Think and What We Can Do about It* (New York: Touchstone, 1990).

Hersch, Patricia. *A Tribe Apart: A Journey into the Heart of American Adolescence* (New York: Ballantine, 1998).

Kindlon, Dan, Ph.D., and Michael Thompson, Ph.D. *Raising Cain: Protecting the Emotional Life of Boys* (New York: Ballantine, 2000).

Kohn, Alfie. *Punished by Rewards: The Trouble with Gold Stars, Incentive Plans, A's, Praise, and Other Bribes* (Boston: Houghton Mifflin, 1993).

Nelsen, Jane, Ed.D., and Cheryl Erwin, M.A. *Parents Who Love Too Much: How Good Parents Can Learn to Love More Wisely and Develop Children of Character* (Rocklin, CA: Prima, 2000).

Nelsen, Jane, Ed.D., Cheryl Erwin, M.A., and Carol Delzer, M.A., J.D. *Positive Discipline for Single Parents: Nurturing, Cooperation, Respect and Joy in Your Single-Parent Family, Revised 2nd Edition* (Rocklin, CA: Prima, 1999).

Nelsen, Jane, Ed.D., Cheryl Erwin, M.A., and Roslyn Duffy. *Positive Discipline: The First Three Years: From Infant to Toddler, 2nd Edition* (New York: Three Rivers Press, 2006).

Nelsen, Jane, Ed.D., and Lynn Lott, M.A. *Positive Discipline A–Z: 1001 Solutions to Everyday Parenting Problems, Revised 3rd Edition.* (New York: Three Rivers Press, 2006).

Pollack, William, Ph.D. *Real Boys: Rescuing Our Sons from the Myths of Boyhood* (New York: Random House, 1998).

Real, Terrence. *I Don't Want to Talk about It: Overcoming the Secret Legacy of Male Depression* (New York: Fireside, 1997).

Ricci, Isolina, Ph.D. *Mom's House, Dad's House: Making Two Homes for Your Child, Revised* (New York: Fireside, 1997).

Shannon, Alice. "Beloved Stranger," *Psychotherapy Networker,* May/June 2005, vol. 29, no. 3, p. 62.

Siegel, Daniel J., M.D. *The Developing Mind: How Relationships and the Brain Interact to Shape Who We Are* (New York: Guilford, 1999).

Siegel, Daniel J., M.D., and Mary Hartzell, M.Ed. *Parenting from the Inside Out: How a Deeper Self-Understanding Can Help You Raise Children Who Thrive* (New York: Jeremy P. Tarcher/Putnam, 2003).

APPENDIX B

Additional Resources

These Web sites are intended for use as general resources and information only. You are your son's parent: Use your good judgment and wisdom about the ideas you encounter.

Parenting Resources
Positive Discipline Association
www.posdis.org

Parents' Action for Children
www.parentsaction.org

Zero to Three
www.zerotothree.org

Tufts University Child & Family Web Guide
www.cfw.tufts.edu

Education and Literacy
Guys Read
www.guysread.com

Child Care
National Association for the Education of Young Children
www.naeyc.org

Child Care Aware
www.childcareaware.org

Media, Violence, and Culture
National Institute on Media and the Family
www.mediafamily.org

Talk with Your Kids
www.talkwithkids.org

Common Sense Media
www.commonsensemedia.org

Development and Health
KidsHealth
www.kidshealth.org

Medline Plus
www.nlm.nih.gov/medlineplus/parenting.html

Child Development Institute
www.childdevelopmentinfo.com

Index